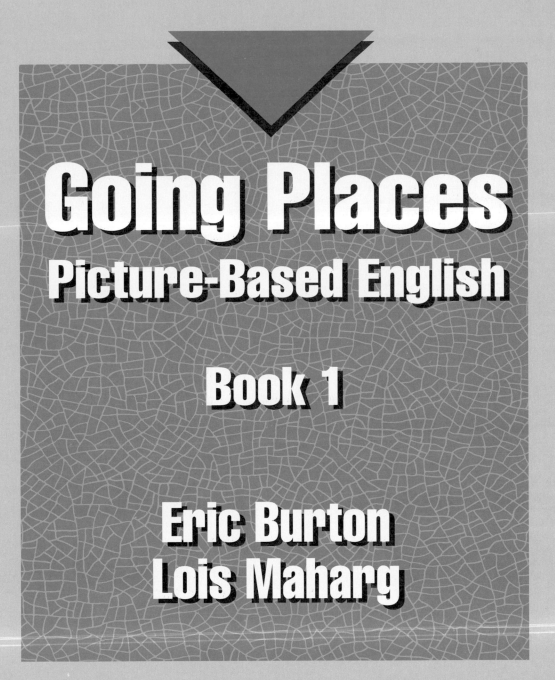

Going Places
Picture-Based English

Book 1

Eric Burton
Lois Maharg

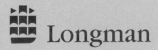
Longman

TO OUR PARENTS

Going Places: Picture-Based English, Book 1

Consultants:
Barry Bakin, *Van Nuys Community Adult School*
Sally Bates, *Long Beach Unified School District*
Sandee Bergman, *New York City Public Schools Adult Ed.*
Yvonne Nishio, *Evans Adult School*
Susan Rabasco, *San Diego Community College, Mid City Adult Center*
April Rice, *West Hills Community College District*
Michael Rost, *Consultant*

A Publication of World Language Division

Associated companies:
Longman Group Ltd., London
Longman Cheshire Pty., Melbourne
Longman Paul Pty., Auckland
Copp Clark Pitman, Toronto

Acquisitions Director: Joanne Dresner
Acquisitions Editor: Anne Boynton-Trigg
Consulting Editor: Michael Rost
Development Editor: Debbie Sistino
Project Manager: Helen B. Ambrosio
Text Design: A Good Thing
Cover Design: Joseph DePinho
Text Art: Tonia and Denman Hampson, Baoping Chen, Woodshed Productions
Production: A Good Thing

Library of Congress Cataloging in Publication Data

Burton, Eric
    Going Places: Picture-based English/Eric Burton and Lois
Maharg
    p. cm.
  ISBN 0-201-82525-2
  1. English language—Textbooks for foreign speakers. I. Maharg,
Lois. II. Title.
PE1128.B848 1995
428.2 4—dc20   94-49596
                              CIP

9 10-CRK-0100

Contents

	LIFE SKILL AREAS	STRUCTURES

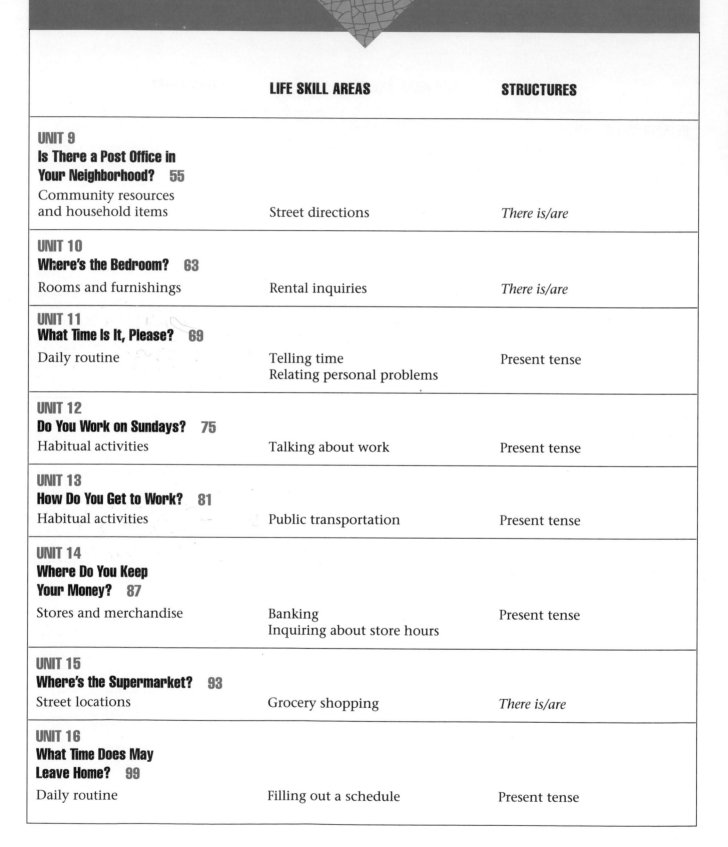

	LIFE SKILL AREAS	STRUCTURES
 Community resources and household items	Street directions	*There is/are*
 Rooms and furnishings	Rental inquiries	*There is/are*
 Daily routine	Telling time Relating personal problems	Present tense
 Habitual activities	Talking about work	Present tense
 Habitual activities	Public transportation	Present tense
 Stores and merchandise	Banking Inquiring about store hours	Present tense
 Street locations	Grocery shopping	*There is/are*
 Daily routine	Filling out a schedule	Present tense

	LIFE SKILL AREAS	STRUCTURES
	Describing interests	Expressions of frequency
	Reporting emergencies	Present tense
	Postal services	Present tense
	First aid	Present tense *vs.* present continuous tense
	Making/registering for doctor's appointments Medical checkup Medical history form	Imperatives
	Medicines	Present tense
	Personal care The calendar	Future *going to*

	LIFE SKILL AREAS	STRUCTURES
UNIT 24 **What's Going to Happen** **Next Monday?** 147		
Predictions	Requesting time off work	Future *going to*
UNIT 25 **Can You Help Me, Please?** 153		
Problems at work	Work schedule changes Requesting assistance	Modal *can*
UNIT 26 **Where Did Maria Go** **Yesterday?** 159		
Past events and Places in Town	Eating out The calendar	Past tense
UNIT 27 **What Did John Do** **Last Week?** 165		
Past events	Calling in sick	Past tense
TAPESCRIPT 170		
TEACHER'S NOTES 184		

INTRODUCTION

Going Places: Picture-Based English is a complete two-level course for beginning ESL students. It is designed to help students develop the practical language they need to function effectively at work, in the community, and in their personal lives. **Going Places** consists of a fully illustrated Student Book, classroom audio cassettes, and a Teacher's Resource Book. The Student Book includes 27 units based on a carefully organized syllabus that integrates topical, life skill, and grammatical strands. The gradual progression of structural elements combined with the unique presentation of practical vocabulary make **Going Places** the ideal course for students beginning their study of English. **Going Places** features:

- pictures *without captions* as a vehicle for introducing and practicing new language

- engaging language presentations through natural, personalized interaction with the teacher

- integration of language structures and functional vocabulary with lifeskill contexts such as shopping, health care and housing

- development of and practice in the four language skills areas of listening, speaking, reading, and writing, progressing in emphasis from reception to production

- opportunities for meaningful, personalized communication using newly acquired language

- lessons that engage students in pair practice and small group interaction

- careful recycling of vocabulary and grammar throughout the book

- a broad range of activities that address various learning styles

- a cultural component in every lesson designed to heighten students' cross-cultural awareness

The Student Book

Each unit in **Going Places 1** follows a consistent format and is taught in three stages. The units begin with the presentation of vocabulary, followed by conversation practice, and end with expansion activities.

I. PRESENTATION OF VOCABULARY

1. Students look at the pictures on the first page of the unit. (They can look at the pictures in their books or on an overhead transparency, if possible.) The teacher presents the new vocabulary by asking personalized, interactive questions about the pictures. The pictures have no captions so students will not be distracted by printed cues and will focus on the oral presentation. At the beginning of each unit, the teacher is referred to the Teacher's Notes at the back of the book. The Teacher's Notes include specific questions and a sample presentation modeling the personalized, interactive questioning technique. For a full discussion of this method for presenting the vocabulary, see page viii in this Introduction.

2. After the initial presentation, students look at the next page of the unit where the pictures are reproduced *with captions*. Students can now see the printed cues as the teacher reviews and clarifies the vocabulary, and models the pronunciation. At this point students are encouraged to repeat the words and phrases, but emphasis is still on reception, not production.

3. Students then practice the vocabulary in pairs, one student reading the vocabulary from page 2 of the unit as the other student points to the appropriate uncaptioned picture on page 1 of the unit. Before the pairwork, the teacher should model this practice with a student, choosing the pictures in random order so students will do the same during the pairwork.

4. Most units include a taped "Listen and Write" activity to reinforce the new vocabulary aurally. (Tapescripts appear in the back of the book.)

5. The conclusion of the vocabulary presentation provides a natural—though not necessary—"breaking off" point for ending a day's lesson, as it gives students a chance to study the new vocabulary at home before proceeding to conversation practice.

II. CONVERSATION PRACTICE

1. The key grammatical structure of the lesson usually appears in a grammar box at the top of the page. The teacher introduces, expands upon,

or reviews the grammar in the context of the new vocabulary.

2. Dialogs in the book related to the pictures on page 1 of the unit incorporate the new vocabulary and the targeted grammatical structure. The teacher models the dialogs and then pairs of students read the dialogs aloud. (Some of the longer dialogs are recorded on tape, as indicated in the text with a cassette symbol.)

3. Now students look again at the uncaptioned pictures on the first page of the unit (in their books or on an OHP). Teacher-student and then student-student pairs model similar dialogs for the class, choosing various pictures. When pairs of students model the dialogs, the teacher should instruct them to alternate roles (asking and answering questions) with each picture, so the class will do the same during pairwork.

4. The class, now practicing in pairs, creates similar dialogs based on the uncaptioned pictures. (To jog students' memories, the teacher can write cues on the chalkboard, and these are suggested in some units.)

5. Much of the conversation pairwork is personalized, with students exchanging information about each other. After such activities, students should be encouraged to share with the whole class things they learned from their partners. This will reinforce the target language, build familiarity among class members, and help the teacher gauge student mastery of the material.

III. EXPANSION ACTIVITIES

The expansion activities in **Going Places** help students achieve lifeskill competencies through listening, speaking, reading, and writing practice. They reinforce the grammatical focus of the unit, review and expand the vocabulary, and further personalize the language students have learned. Expansion activities fall into five categories:

Writing activities—Students write sentences to reinforce and expand the language they have practiced orally. In most cases, students are instructed to write about themselves and should be encouraged to share one or more sentences with the rest of the class.

Listening activities—Students listen to taped conversations and demonstrate comprehension by completing a task (ordering, matching, and so on). In some cases, students then write sentences or create and practice dialogs based on the listening

exercises. (Tapescripts for all conversations appear in the back of the book.)

Reading activities—Students read dialogs or stories and demonstrate comprehension by completing a task. In some cases, students then write sentences or create and practice dialogs based on the reading.

Information gap speaking activities—Students work in pairs, each partner looking at a different page, and ask and answer questions about information on their partner's page.

Culture questions—Students and teacher discuss cultural differences and similarities relating to the topic of the unit.

Note: **Going Places** features boldfacing of selected vocabulary and expressions appearing *for the first time* so the teacher can clarify, if necessary. Salient structural elements are also boldfaced so students will take note.

The Teacher's Resource Book

The Teacher's Resource Book provides detailed step-by-step procedures for key exercises and additional teaching suggestions for each lesson. Sample language presentations for introducing the pictures on the first page of every unit are also included. In addition, the Teacher's Resource Book features:

- reproducible grammar exercises
- expansion activities for every unit

Presenting New Vocabulary through Pictures

On the first page of each unit, teachers are referred to a page in the Teacher's Notes that lists questions to ask while presenting the pictures on that page, and includes an example of how the presentation of the page might start out. Specific teaching tips are also given for selected units. Teachers are urged to read the notes before starting each unit, although with time they may find it unnecessary to refer to the sample presentations. (Additional, more detailed suggestions for carrying out each lesson are provided in the Teacher's Resource Book.)

Below are guidelines for presenting the vocabulary through pictures.

1. The key to successfully presenting the first page of each unit is to create a *natural, personal interaction* between yourself and your students that will keep them continually responding and thus actively engaged.

2. During the presentation, the students look at the pictures on the first page of the unit in their books or on an overhead transparency, if possible. *(You* will be looking at the page in the Teacher's Notes that offers teaching suggestions.)

3. Build the presentation around simple *yes/no* and "choice" questions, e.g.:

   "Do we cook food in the bathroom?"

   "Do we wear coats when it's *hot,* or when it's *cold*?"

4. As you ask the questions, use words your students are already familiar with and personalize the new vocabulary by relating it to their lives. (See examples below.) It is not necessary to limit yourself strictly to language that has already been presented in the book, however, since students' receptive abilities are greater than their productive skills.

5. Do not answer your own questions. When necessary, do the following to help students understand and answer your questions:
   a. use pantomime
   b. point to clues in the pictures
   c. use "give-away" questions, e.g.,
      "Is this a *toothbrush,* or a *hammer*?"
      "Do we *cook* with a microwave, or *wash clothes* with a microwave?"
   d. simply feed students answers, e.g.,

   "Who's wearing a *shirt* in this class? [no answer from students} . . . Well, is Peter wearing a shirt? [touching Peter's shirt] . . . Yes, Peter's wearing a shirt. And who else? . . ."

6. Use each new vocabulary item in several questions as you present it. Also, skip around the page and review frequently to reinforce and check students' retention of items already presented. For example,
   "Which picture has the ___[bank]___?"
   "Point to the picture of the ___[hammer]___."

7. Have students keep their pencils down and notebooks closed during the presentation, to keep their focus on the *oral* interaction. (Reassure them that the new vocabulary is in their books for later reference.) During the presentation, you can write new vocabulary items on the chalkboard as they are introduced, *and then erase them after a few moments*. This will give students a "visual take" on the new words, while maintaining the focus on the oral presentation.

8. Adjust the pacing and the length (amount of repetition) of your presentation to your students' abilities and the difficulty of the lesson. A presentation may last between 20 and 40 minutes.

9. During the presentation, be concerned primarily that students *understand* the new vocabulary, not that they be able to produce it.

The following examples offer a general idea of what a presentation might sound like:

1. *Picture being presented: a blouse* (from Unit 3)

Teacher's presentation: Is this a blouse or a banana? . . . It's a blouse, a blouse. Who wears a blouse, a man or a woman? . . . A woman wears a blouse. Who has a blouse on in this class? . . . Tran does. What color is Tran's blouse? . . . Her blouse is white. Is a blouse always white? . . . No, a blouse can also be other colors. Is that a new blouse or an old one, Tran? . . . A new one? Where did you buy it—at Macy's? Downtown? In Chinatown? . . .

2. *Picture being presented: clean the house* (from Unit 6)

Teacher's presentation: Who's in this picture? . . . It's John. What's he doing here? Is he teaching a lesson? . . . No, he isn't teaching a lesson. So what's he doing? . . . He's cleaning. And what is he cleaning—his car or his house? . . . Yes, he's cleaning his house. What about you, Phuong, do you clean your house sometimes? . . . You do? And do you *like* to clean your house? . . . No, you don't like to clean your house. Me neither! I don't like to clean my house. And *when* do you usually clean your house, Phuong? At night? On the weekends? . . . Oh, you usually clean your house on Sunday. What about you, Natalia? When do you clean your house? . . . What? You don't clean your house?! . . . Oh, I see. Your *husband* cleans your house.

English for the Classroom

1. Learn the new words. Repeat the words after your teacher.

①

Listen.

②

Look at the chalkboard.

③

Write the words.

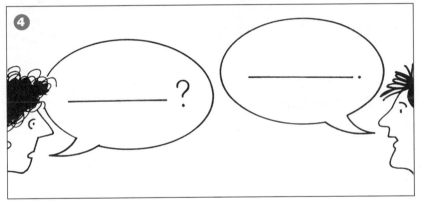

④

Ask a question.

Answer.
Answer the question.

⑤

Read the sentence.

⑥

Repeat.

⑦

Continue. / Go on. / Next.

⑧

Study Unit 1.

Topic: the classroom
Life skills: following directions
  asking questions in class
Structures: imperatives; plurals

2. Match the pictures and words.

1. Read the sentence.

2. Listen.

3. Continue.

4. Ask a question.

5. Write the words.

6. Look at the chalkboard.

7. Study Unit 1.

8. Repeat.

9. Answer the question.

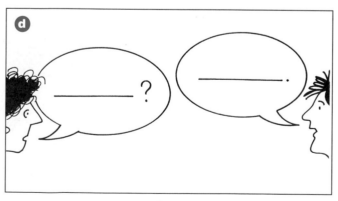

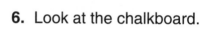

Teacher, see page 184 for additional activities to reinforce this vocabulary.

3. Learn the new words. Look at the pictures. Repeat the words after your teacher.

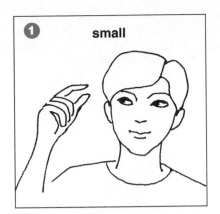

1 small

What does this mean?
What is the meaning?

2 small

How do you say this word?

3 small

big

opposite

4 small

s-m-a-l-l

How do you spell it?
What is the spelling?

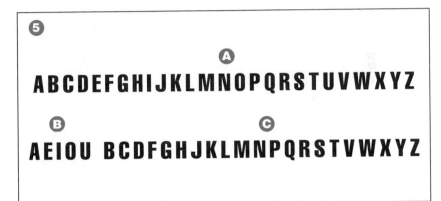

5

Ⓐ

ABCDEFGHIJKLMNOPQRSTUVWXYZ

Ⓑ   Ⓒ

AEIOU BCDFGHJKLMNPQRSTVWXYZ

A. 26 letters in the alphabet   B. 5 vowels   C. 21 consonants

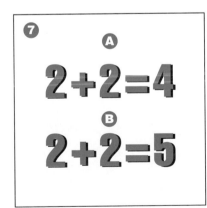

6
Ⓐ
book
Ⓑ
books

A. singular
B. plural

7
Ⓐ
2+2=4
Ⓑ
2+2=5

A. right
B. wrong

8
Ⓐ
Ⓑ

A. I don't understand.
B. I understand.

4. **Match the questions and answers.**

DESK

1. How many vowels?

2. How many consonants?

3. What is the first consonant?

4. What is the last consonant?

BIG

5. What does it mean?

6. How do you say it?

7. How do you spell it?

8. What is the opposite?

BOOK

9. Singular or plural?

BOOKS

10. Singular or plural?

Ⓐ small

Ⓑ three

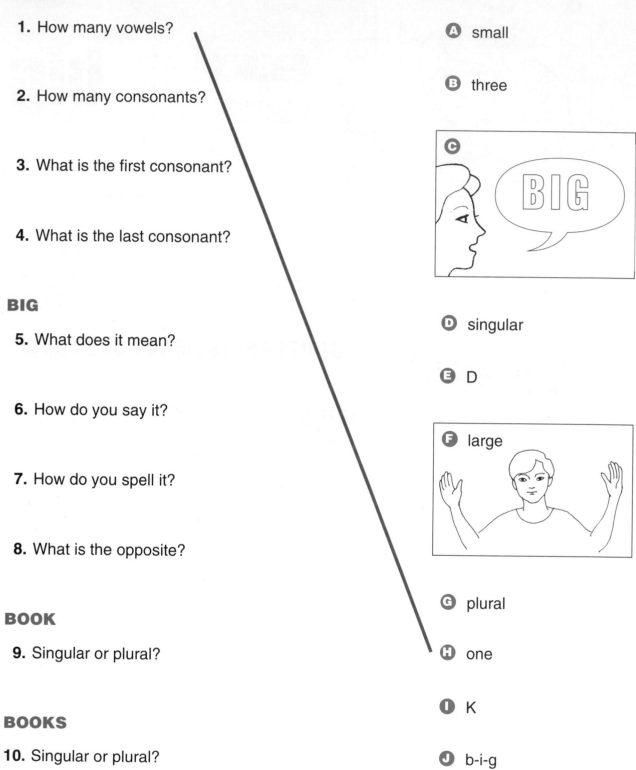

Ⓒ

Ⓓ singular

Ⓔ D

Ⓕ large

Ⓖ plural

Ⓗ one

Ⓘ K

Ⓙ b-i-g

Teacher, see page 184 for additional activities to reinforce this vocabulary.

Plurals

1. Read the words. Repeat them after your teacher.

Singular	Plural
a book	books
an apple	apples
a box	boxes
a dish	dishes
an inch	inches
a bus	buses
a baby	babies

↑ ——— *consonant*

a boy	boys

↑ ——— *vowel*

a person	people ⎤
a child	children
a man	men
a woman	women *irregular words*
a foot	feet
a tooth	teeth ⎦

a book	an apple
a dish	an eye

Write the plurals.

1. book_____

2. person_____

3. day_____

4. dish_____

5. foot_____

6. desk_____

7. baby_____

8. face_____

9. class_____

10. woman_____

11. hand_____

12. eye_____

13. watch_____

14. bus_____

15. child_____

16. box _____

17. apple _____

18. man_____

Now say the words with your teacher and classmates.

Introductions

John, Maria, and Stan are friends.

They all work in the same school.

Mr. Morgan is their boss.

Introductions

At Home

This is John and his wife, May.

They have three children—Tim, Kate, and Baby Ben.

Zabu is their dog.

What's Your First Name?

1. Look at the pictures. Answer your teacher's questions. **(Teacher, see page 184.)**

① Maria Lopez

② 3340 Park St., apt. 4
Los Angeles, California
90436

③ (213) 555-2228

④ SOCIAL SECURITY
123-45-6789

⑤ 12 92

⑥ 3-15-69

⑦

⑧

⑨

Topic: personal information
Life skill: filling out forms
Structure: *to be*; ordinal numbers

9

Asking Personal Information

2. Learn the new words. Listen to the questions. Repeat them after your teacher.

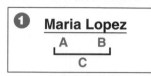

❶ Maria Lopez

A   B

C

1. What's your name?
   A. What's your first name?
   B. What's your last name?
   C. What's your full name?

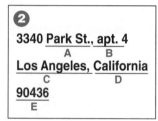

❷

3340 Park St., apt. 4
A   B

Los Angeles, California
C   D

90436
E

2. Where do you live? *or*
   What's your address?
   A. What street do you live on?
   B. What's your
      apartment number?
   C. What city do you live in?
   D. What state do you live in?
   E. What's your zip code?

❸

(213) 555-2228
A   B

3. A. What's your area code?
   B. What's your telephone number?

❹

123-45-6789

4. What's your social security number?

❺   12   92

5. How old are you? *or*
   What's your age?

❻

3-15-69
A   B

6. When's your birthday? *or*
   When were you born?
   A. What month were you born?
   B. What year were you born?

❼

7. Where are you from? *or*
   Where do you come from? *or*
   Where were you born?

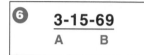

❽

8. Are you married or single?

❾

9. What do you do? *or*
   What's your job?

PAIRWORK. Practice with a partner. Student A, look at this page and ask questions. Student B, look at page 9 and point to the pictures.

3. Listen and number the pictures.

(213) 555-2228

1

3-15-69

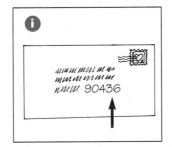

SOCIAL SECURITY

123-45-6789

3340 Park St., apt. 4
Los Angeles, California
90436

90436

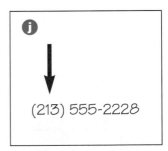

(213) 555-2228

4. Your teacher will ask you the questions from page 10. Answer about yourself.

Dates

5. Learn the new words. Listen to the dates. Repeat them after your teacher.

❶ **Jan.** **1**
January first

❷ **Feb.** **2**
February second

❸ **Mar.** **3**
March third

❹ **April** **4**
April fourth

❺ **May** **5**
May fifth

❻ **June** **9**
June ninth

❼ **July** **12**
July twelfth

❽ **Aug.** **20**
August twentieth

❾ **Sept.** **21**
September twenty-first

❿ **Oct.** **22**
October twenty-second

⓫ **Nov.** **23**
November twenty-third

⓬ **Dec.** **30**
December thirtieth

Learn about Your Classmates

6. Ask six classmates their first names and birthdays. Write the answers below.

Classmate's Name	Birthday
1.	
2.	
3.	
4.	
5.	
6.	

7. Learn about John and Maria. Listen and answer your teacher's questions.

For example: What's his name?
What's her phone number?
What state does he live in?
Where is she from?

John Phillips
257 Lake Ave.
Los Angeles, California 90485
(213) 555-4668
SS# 987-65-4321
July 25, 1950, Homer, New York

Lopez , Maria
3340 Park St., #4
Los Angeles, California 90436
(213) 555-2228
SS# 123-45-6789
March 15, 1969, Dallas, Texas

Giving Personal Information

8. Learn the new words. Listen to the answers. Repeat them after your teacher.

❶ **Maria Lopez**
A   B
C

1. My name is Maria Lopez.
   A. My name is Maria.
   B. My last name is Lopez.

❷
3340 Park St., apt. 4
A   B
Los Angeles, California
C   D
90436
E

2. My address is 3340 Park Street. *or*
   I live at 3340 Park Street.
   A. I live on Park Street.
   B. I live in apartment 4.
   C. I live in Los Angeles.
   D. I live in California.
   E. My zip code is 90436.

❸ **(213) 555-2228**
A   B

3. **A.** My area code is 213.
   B. My telephone number
       is 555-2228.

❹ **123-45-6789**

4. My social security number is
   123-45-6789.

❺    I'm = I am

5. I'm 12.
   I'm 92 years old.

❻ **3-15-69**
A   B

6. My birthday is March 15.
   A. I was born in March.
   B. I was born in 1969.

❼

7. I'm from the United States. *or*
   I was born in the United States.

❽

8. I'm married.
   I'm single.
   I'm **divorced**.

❾

9. I'm a ____ *teacher* ____.

PAIRWORK. Practice with a partner. Student A, look at this page and say the sentences. Student B, look at page 9 and point to the pictures.

9. Ask six classmates their names, telephone numbers, and streets. Write the answers below.

Classmate's Name	Telephone Number	Street
1.		
2.		
3.		
4.		
5.		
6.		

10. Practice the conversations with your teacher.

A: How old are you?

B: I'm _____ . How about you?

A: I'm _____ .

A: Where are you from?

B: I'm from _____ . How about you?

A: _____ .

(213) 555-2228

A: What's your telephone number?

B: My telephone number is _____ . How about you?

A: _____ .

PAIRWORK. Now look at page 9. Make new conversations with a partner.

How do you greet people in your country?

Filling Out a Form

11. Look at the form with your teacher. Then write the information. Please **print**.

Name _____

            last   first   **m.i.**

Address _____

         street   apt. no.

_____

         city   state   zip

Telephone (_____) _____

Social security no. _____

Sex: ❏ M   ❏ F

Date of Birth _____ / _____ / _____ Age _____

Place of Birth _____

Marital status: ❏ single ❏ married ❏ divorced ❏ **widowed**

Occupation _____

Signature _____

Where's John?

1. Look at the pictures. Answer your teacher's questions. (Teacher, see page 184.)

John

Maria

Tony and Mark

Jane

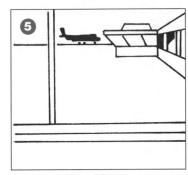
Mr. and Mrs. Morgan

Lee and Peter

Tim and Kate

Ann

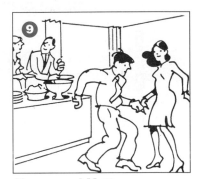
Nancy and Matt

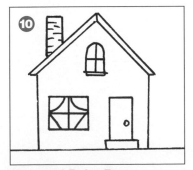
May and Baby Ben

Pablo

Tom

Topic: **places in town**
Life skill: **grocery shopping**
Structure: *to be*

17

Places around Town

2. Learn the new words. Listen to the words. Repeat them after your teacher.

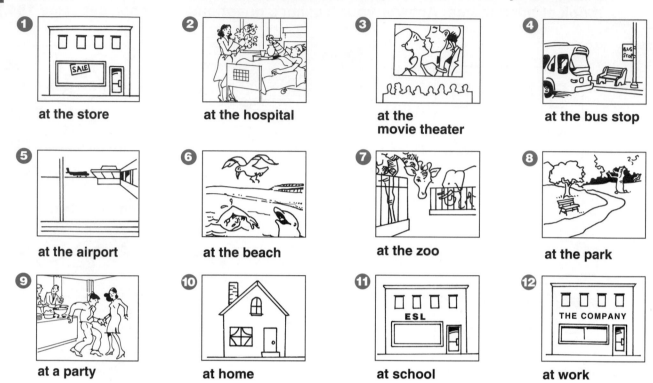

1. at the store
2. at the hospital
3. at the movie theater
4. at the bus stop
5. at the airport
6. at the beach
7. at the zoo
8. at the park
9. at a party
10. at home
11. at school
12. at work

PAIRWORK. Practice with a partner. Student A, look at this page and say the words. Student B, look at page 17 and point to the pictures.

Listen and Write

3. Listen and complete the sentences.

1. Pablo is at ___school___.

2. Mr. and Mrs. Morgan are at _____ _____.

3. Ann is at _____ _____.

4. Tony and Mark are at _____ _____ _____.

5. Nancy and Matt are at _____ _____.

6. Jane is at _____ _____ _____.

7. May and Baby Ben are at _____.

8. Maria is at _____ _____.

Conversation

Where**'s** John?	He**'s** at _____ .
Where**'s** Maria?	She**'s** at _____ .
Where **are** Tony and Mark?	They**'re** at _____ .

's = is
're = are

4. Listen to the conversation. Then practice it with your teacher.

A: Where's Pablo?
B: He's at school.

A: Where's Ann?
B: She's at the park.

A: Where are Lee and Peter?
B: They're at the beach.

PAIRWORK. Now look at page 17. Make new conversations with a partner.

Conversation

| Who's at _____ ? |

5. Practice the conversations with your teacher.

A: Who's at school?
B: Pablo (is).

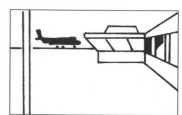

A: Who's at the airport?
B: Mr. and Mrs. Morgan (are).

PAIRWORK. Now look at page 17. Make new conversations with a partner.

husband   wife   daughter   son

brother   sister   mother   father

Writing Practice

6. Write where your family and friends are now.

Example: My husband is at work. _____

1. _____

2. _____

3. _____

4. _____

At the Store

 7. Learn the new words. Look at the pictures.
Repeat the words after your teacher.
Then listen to John's conversation with the **clerk**.
Draw a line from the food to the **correct** aisle.

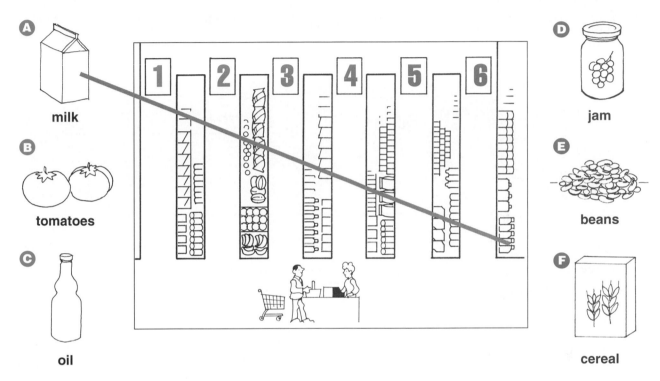

A milk

B tomatoes

C oil

D jam

E beans

F cereal

8. Practice the conversations with your teacher.

A: Where's the milk?
B: On aisle 6.

A: Where are the tomatoes?
B: On aisle 1.

PAIRWORK. Now look at the pictures again. Make new conversations with a partner.

Are food stores in your country big or small?

Food Containers

9. Learn the new words. Look at the pictures. Repeat the words after your teacher.

| bottle | can | jar | box |

10. Look at the pictures. Write the missing words.

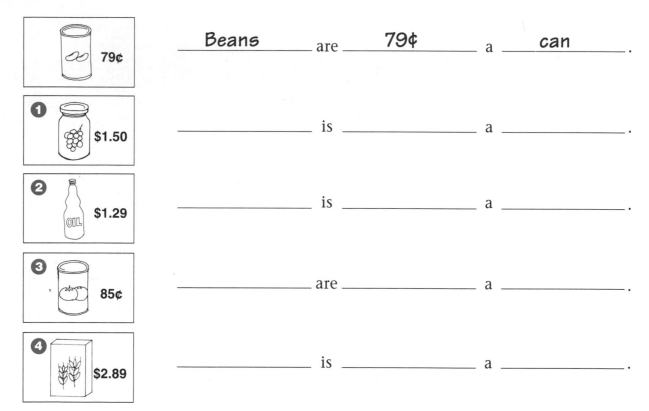

_____Beans_____ are _____79¢_____ a _____can_____ .

79¢

① $1.50

_____ is _____ a _____ .

② OIL $1.29

_____ is _____ a _____ .

③ 85¢

_____ are _____ a _____ .

④ $2.89

_____ is _____ a _____ .

11. What foods do you buy by the bottle, by the can, by the jar, and by the box? With your teacher and your classmates, write the names of foods on the lines below.

bottle	can	jar	box
_____	_____	_____	_____
_____	_____	_____	_____
_____	_____	_____	_____
_____	_____	_____	_____
_____	_____	_____	_____

What Size Is the Shirt?

1. Look at the pictures. Answer your teacher's questions. **(Teacher, see page 184.)**

① $19 — L

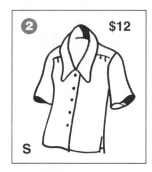
② $12 — S

③ $18 — M

④ $24.99 — L

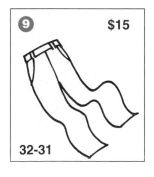
⑤ $3.99 — 34

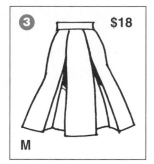
⑥ 2/$8

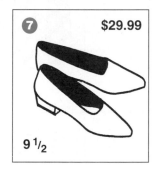
⑦ $29.99 — 9 ½

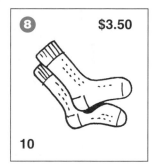
⑧ $3.50 — 10

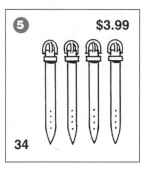
⑨ $15 — 32-31

⑩ $6 — XL

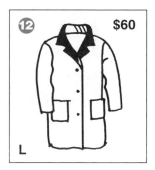
⑪ $8.95 — M

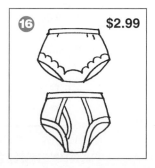
⑫ $60 — L

⑬ $39 — M

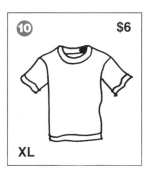
⑭ $4.99 — S

⑮ $22 — P

⑯ $2.99

Topic: clothing items
Life skill: clothes shopping
Structure: *to be*

Clothes

2. Learn the new words. Listen to the words. Repeat them after your teacher.

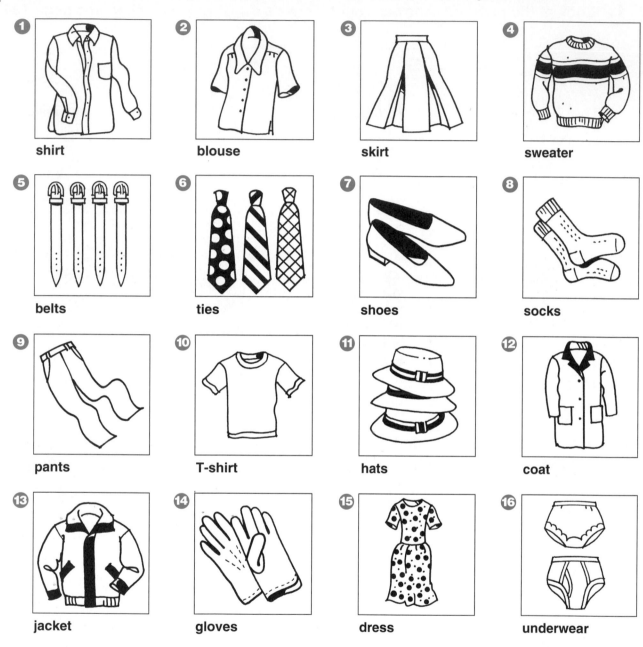

① shirt

② blouse

③ skirt

④ sweater

⑤ belts

⑥ ties

⑦ shoes

⑧ socks

⑨ pants

⑩ T-shirt

⑪ hats

⑫ coat

⑬ jacket

⑭ gloves

⑮ dress

⑯ underwear

SIZES
P = Petite S = Small M = Medium L = Large XL = Extra Large
Pants: 32 inches (waist)   31 inches (length)

PAIRWORK. Practice with a partner. Student A, look at this page and say the names of the clothes. Student B, look at page 23 and point to the pictures.

3. **Listen to the sentences. Repeat them after your teacher.**

Example: 9½ — nine and a half

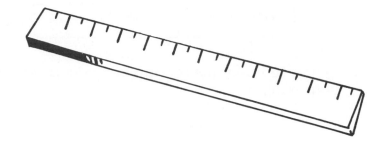

1. My class is 2½ hours long.

2. I work 8½ hours every day.

3. My shoes are size 10½.

4. I walk 3½ miles to school.

5. My son is 6½ years old.

4. **Listen to the prices. Repeat them after your teacher.**

Examples: $4.50 – four and a half dollars *or*
four dollars and fifty cents *or*
four fifty

$3.25 – three dollars and twenty-five cents *or*
three twenty-five

1. $19.50	2. $9.95	3. $24.49	4. $55.50
5. $17.76	6. $62.80	7. $81.65	8. $30.20

5. **Listen to the prices. Repeat them after your teacher.**

Examples: $125 – one hundred and twenty-five dollars *or*
a hundred and twenty-five dollars

$899 – eight hundred and ninety-nine dollars

$1,000 – one thousand dollars *or*
a thousand dollars

$3,500 – three thousand five hundred dollars

1. $6,900	2. $225	3. $595	4. $1,450
5. $124	6. $3,716	7. $1,112	8. $862

PAIRWORK. Student A, read a number. Student B, close your book. Write the number.

Conversation

How much	is	the _____?	It's _____.
What size	are		They're _____.

6. Listen to the conversation between May and the clerk. Then practice it with your teacher.

Clerk: Can I help you?
May: Yes, please. How much is the skirt?
Clerk: It's $18.00.
May: What size is it?
Clerk: Medium.
May: I'll take it.

May: How much are the shoes?
Clerk: They're $29.99.
May: What size are they?
Clerk: They're size 9^1/$_2$.

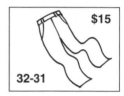

May: And how much are the pants?
Clerk: They're $15.00.
May: Thank you.

PAIRWORK. Now look at page 23. Make new conversations with a partner.

Listen and Write

7. John is talking with a salesclerk. Read the questions. Then listen to each conversation. After you listen, write the answers.

Conversation 1: What size is the blouse? _____

Conversation 2: What size is the skirt? _____

Conversation 3: How much is the dress? _____

Conversation 4: What color is the jacket? _____

| red | orange | yellow | green | blue | pink | black | gray | brown | white |

Shopping

INFORMATION GAP. Work with a partner. Student A, look at this page. Student B, look at page 28.

8. Look at the pictures. Ask Student B about the men's clothing. Write the **information.** Then answer Student B's questions about the women's clothing.

Men's Clothing

Price: _____	Price: _____
Size: _____	Size: _____
Color: _____	Color: _____

Women's Clothing

$12.95	$18.00
6, 8, 10, 12	7, 9, 11, 13
red, green, yellow	blue

Price: _____	Price: _____
Size: _____	Size: _____
Color: _____	Color: _____

$1.99	$5.50
5, 6, 7	S, M, L
white, pink, blue	black, brown

 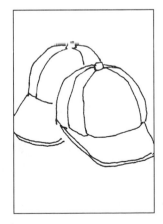 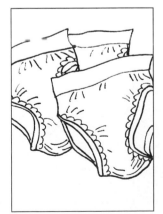 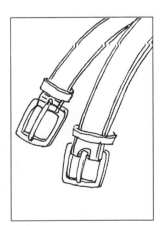

 Is clothing more expensive in your country or in the United States?

INFORMATION GAP. Work with a partner. Student B, look at this page.
Student A, look at page 27.

8. Look at the pictures. Answer Student A's questions about the men's clothing.
Then ask Student A about the women's clothing. Write the **information**.

Men's Clothing

Women's Clothing

$24.99

$9.79

Price: _____

Price: _____

M, L, XL

S, M, L

Size: _____

Size: _____

blue

green, brown

Color: _____

Color: _____

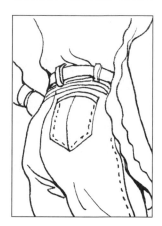

$1.50

$4.95

Price: _____

Price: _____

8, 9, 10

M

Size: _____

Size: _____

black, gray, white

red, blue

Color: _____

Color: _____

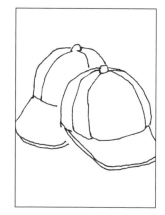
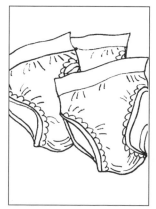
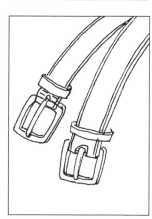

 Is clothing more expensive in your country or in the United States?

UNIT 4 · Where's Zabu?

1. Look at the pictures. Answer your teacher's questions. **(Teacher, see page 185.)**

Topic: locations
Life skills: department store shopping; kitchen items
Structure: prepositions of location

29

Locations

2. Learn the new words. Repeat them after your teacher.

1
inside his house
or in his house

2
outside his house

3
in the corner

4
around his house

5
over his house
or above his house

6
under his house
or below his house

7
in front of
his house

8
in back of his house
or behind his house

9
on top of his house

10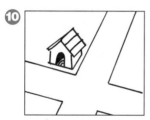
at the corner

11
next to his house
or beside his house

12
between the houses

PAIRWORK. Practice with a partner. Student A, look at this page and say the words. Student B, look at page 29 and point to the pictures.

Listen and Write

 3. Listen to the names of the **shapes.** Repeat them after your teacher.

circle   square   triangle

Now listen and write the letters.

Conversation

4. Practice the conversations with your teacher.

A: Where's Zabu?
B: He's beside his house.

A: Where's Zabu?
B: He's behind his house.

A: Where's Zabu?
B: He's under his house.

PAIRWORK. Now look at page 29. Make new conversations with a partner.

Is Zabu _____ ?	**Yes,** he is. **No,** he isn't.

isn't = is not

5. Practice the conversations with your teacher.

A: Is Zabu behind his house?
B: No, he isn't.
A: Is he on top of his house?
B: Yes, he is.

PAIRWORK. Now look at page 29. Make new conversations with a partner.

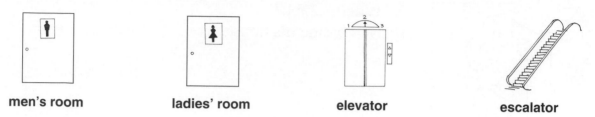

At the Department Store

6. Learn the new words. Look at the pictures. Repeat the words after your teacher. Then practice the conversation.

men's room   ladies' room   elevator   escalator

Maria: Excuse me. Where is the ladies' room?
Clerk: It's on the second floor next to the elevator.
Maria: Thank you.
Clerk: You're welcome.

7. Listen to the conversations. Draw a line from the picture to the correct location.

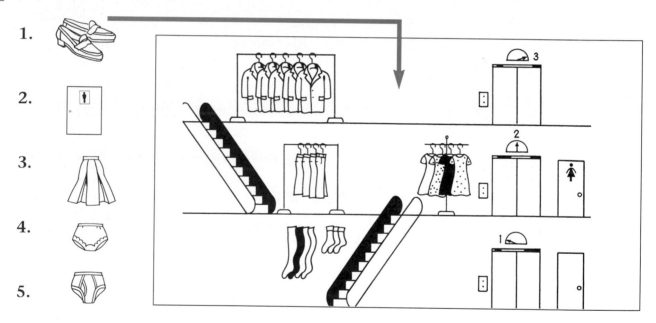

1.

2.

3.

4.

5.

8. Write sentences.

1. ___Men's shoes are on the third floor beside the coats.___

2. _____

3. _____

4. _____

5. _____

Where's the Knife?

9. Look at the picture. Answer your teacher's questions. **(Teacher, see page 185.)**

Things in the Kitchen

10. Learn the new words. Listen to the words. Repeat them after your teacher.

1 spoon **2** knife **3** fork **4** sponge **5** counter **6** shelf

7 dish **8** bowl **9** glass **10** cup **11** pot **12** pan

PAIRWORK. Now practice with a partner. Student A, look at this page and say the words. Student B, look at page 33 and point to the pictures.

Conversation

11. Practice the conversations with your teacher.

A: Where's the sponge?
B: It's next to the bowl.

A: Where are the forks?
B: They're on the dishes.

Are the _____ ?	Yes, they **are.**	**aren't = are not**
	No, they **aren't.**	

12. Practice the conversation with your teacher.

A: Are the glasses on the counter?
B: No, they aren't.
A: Are the glasses on the shelf?
B: Yes, they are.

PAIRWORK. Now look at page 33. Make new conversations with a partner. Follow the conversations in exercises 11 and 12.

 Do people in your country eat with forks and spoons?

What's John Doing?

1. Look at the pictures. Answer your teacher's questions. (Teacher, see page 185.)

John

Baby Ben

Tony and Mark

Jane

Mr. and Mrs. Morgan

Lee and Peter

Maria

Ann

Tom and Sue

Tim and Kate

Pablo

Nancy and Matt

Topic: activities in town
Life skill: school facilities
Structure: present continuous

35

Activities around Town

2. Learn the new words. Listen to the words. Repeat them after your teacher.

① school
teach a lesson

② home
sleep

③ theater
watch a movie

④ bus stop
wait for the bus

⑤ airport
meet a friend

⑥ beach
swim

⑦ hospital
visit a friend

⑧ park
run

⑨ store
buy food

⑩ zoo
look at the animals

⑪ work
drive a truck

⑫ party
dance

PAIRWORK. Practice with a partner. Student A, look at this page and say the words. Student B, look at page 35 and point to the pictures.

Listen and Write

Use *-ing* to talk about right now.

3. Listen and complete the sentences.

1. John is _____teaching_____ a lesson to his class.

2. Mr. and Mrs. Morgan are _____ing a friend at the airport.

3. Baby Ben is _____ing at home.

4. Jane is _____ing for the bus.

5. Maria is _____ing a friend at the hospital.

6. Tom and Sue are _____ing food at the store.

7. Tony and Mark are _____ing a movie at the theater.

Conversation

Who's _____ ing?

4. Listen to the conversation. Then practice it with your teacher.

A: Who's driving the truck?
B: Tom is.

A: Who's dancing?
B: Nancy and Matt are.

PAIRWORK. Now look at page 35. Make new conversations with a partner.

What's	he	doing?
	she	
What are they doing?		

5. Practice the conversations with your teacher.

A: Where's John?
B: At school.
A: What's he doing?
B: Teaching a lesson.

A: Where are Mr. and Mrs. Morgan?
B: At the airport.
A: What are they doing?
B: Meeting a friend.

PAIRWORK. Now look at page 35. Make new conversations with a partner.

Spelling

| A. buy ⟶ buying <br> wait ⟶ waiting | B. live ⟶ living <br> take ⟶ taking | C. swim ⟶ swimming
 ↑↑ 1 consonant
 ↑ 1 vowel <br> run ⟶ running
 ↑↑ 1 consonant
 ↑ 1 vowel |

6. Add *-ing* to these words. Follow the examples above.

1. read _____

2. study _____

3. write _____

4. look _____

5. dance _____

6. teach _____

7. drive _____

8. stop _____

9. sit _____

Learn about Your Classmates

7. Practice the conversations with your teacher.

A: Where's your sister now?
B: At home.
A: What's she doing?
B: **Maybe** sleeping.

A: Where are your children now?
B: I don't have children.

PAIRWORK. Now close your book and ask some classmates about people in their families.

8. Write what people in your family are doing now.

Example: ___My mother is cooking dinner.___

1. _____

2. _____

3. _____

4. _____

 Are there many zoos in your country? Are there many theaters?

At School

INFORMATION GAP. Work with a partner. Student A, look at this page.
Student B, look at page 40.

9. Learn the new words. Look at the picture below. Repeat these words after
your teacher.

hall   office   listening lab   restroom

10. Practice the conversations with your partner.

A: Where's John?
B: He's in room 100.
A: What's he doing?
B: Teaching a lesson.

A: Where's Jane?
B: She's in the hall.
A: What's she doing?
B: Buying coffee.

Look at the school building. Ask Student B about Mark, Sue, and Ann and draw a
line from the name to the correct room. Then answer Student B's questions.

11. Write the answers.

1. What's John doing? _____Teaching a lesson._____

2. What's Jane doing? _____

3. What's Mark doing? _____

4. What's Sue doing? _____

5. What's Ann doing? _____

INFORMATION GAP. Work with a partner. Student B, look at this page. Student A, look at page 39.

9. Learn the new words. Look at the picture below. Repeat these words after your teacher.

hall   office   listening lab   restroom

10. Practice the conversations with your partner.

A: Where's John?

B: He's in room 100.

A: What's he doing?

B: Teaching a lesson.

A: Where's Jane?

B: She's in the hall.

A: What's she doing?

B: Buying coffee.

Look at the school building. Answer Student A's questions. Then ask Student A about Maria, Lee, and Zabu and draw a line to the correct room.

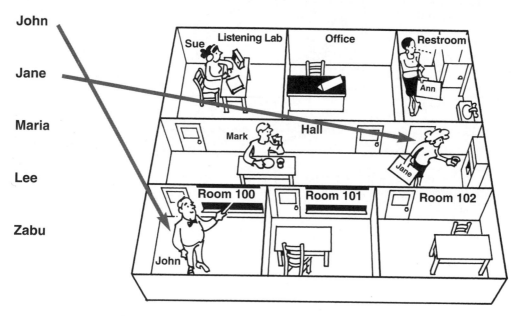

11. Write the answers.

1. What's John doing? _____ Teaching a lesson. _____

2. What's Jane doing? _____

3. What's Maria doing? _____

4. What's Lee doing? _____

5. What's Zabu doing? _____

Who's Cleaning the House?

1. Look at the pictures. Answer your teacher's questions. **(Teacher, see page 186.)**

John

Nancy and Matt

Mr. and Mrs. Morgan

Stan

Maria

Ann

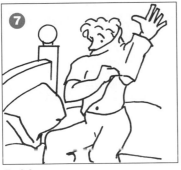

Pablo

Mark

Peter

Lee

Tony

Tom and Sue

Topic: activities at home
Life skill: talking about family
Structure: present continuous

41

Activities at Home

2. Learn the new words. Listen to the words. Repeat them after your teacher.

1 clean the house

2 sleep

3 wash the dishes

4 cook a meal

5 fill out a form

6 write a letter

7 get dressed

8 get undressed

9 drink coffee

10 take a shower

11 take a bath

12 They aren't doing anything.

PAIRWORK. Practice with a partner. Student A, look at this page and say the words. Student B, look at page 41 and point to the pictures.

Listen and Write

3. Listen and complete the questions.

1. Who's _____taking_____ a shower?   Lee is.

2. Who's _____ a meal?   Stan is.

3. Who's _____ dressed?   Pablo is.

4. Who's _____ a letter?   Ann is.

5. Who's _____ coffee?   Peter is.

6. Who's _____ the house?   John is.

PAIRWORK. Now look at page 41. Ask and answer *Who* questions with a partner.

Talk and Write

4. Look at the pictures. Read the sentences. Make new sentences with your teacher. Then write the sentences.

He She	is isn't	_____ ing.
They	are aren't	

Ann

1. Ann is writing a letter.

2. She isn't filling out a form.

Nancy and Matt

3. Nancy and Matt are sleeping.

4. They aren't cleaning the house.

Pablo

5. Pablo _____

6. _____

Mr. and Mrs. Morgan

7. Mr. and Mrs. Morgan _____

8. _____

5. PAIRWORK. Look at page 35 and tell what the people are doing.

Examples: Mr. and Mrs. Morgan are meeting a friend at the airport.
Baby Ben is sleeping at home.

Conversation

Is	he / she	_____ing?	Yes, she/he is. No, she/he isn't. (No, she's/he's not.)
Are they			Yes, they are. No, they aren't. (No, they're not.)

 6. Listen to the conversation. Then practice it with your teacher.

A: Is Ann writing a letter?
B: Yes, she is.

A: Is Pablo taking a shower?
B: No, he isn't. *or* No, he's not.

A: Are Nancy and Matt sleeping?
B: Yes, they are.

A: Are Mr. and Mrs. Morgan cooking a meal?
B: No, they aren't. *or* No, they're not.

PAIRWORK. Now look at the pictures on page 41. Make new conversations with a partner.

7. Practice the sentences with your teacher.

1. Right now my sister is cleaning the house.

2. My mother and father are watching TV at home now.

3. My husband isn't doing anything now.

PAIRWORK. Close your book. Tell a partner what your family is doing right now.

Who cleans the house in your family? Who cooks the meals?

Why Is John Crying?

1. Look at the pictures. Answer your teacher's questions. **(Teacher, see page 186.)**

John

Tim and Kate

Baby Ben

May

Maria

Zabu

Topic: feelings
Life skill: inquiring about family
Structure: present continuous

45

Feelings

2. Learn the new words. Listen to the words. Repeat them after your teacher.

① cry
sad

② argue
angry

③ yawn
tired

④ bite (her) nails
worried

⑤ scratch (her) head
confused

⑥ bark
scared

PAIRWORK. Practice with a partner. Student A, look at this page and say the words. Student B, look at page 45 and point to the pictures.

Conversation

Why	is	he she	_____ ing?
	are	they	

3. Practice the conversation with your teacher.

A: Who's crying ?
B: John is.
A: **Why** is he crying?
B: **Because** he's sad.

A: Who's arguing?
B: Tim and Kate are.
A: Why are they arguing?
B: Because they're angry.

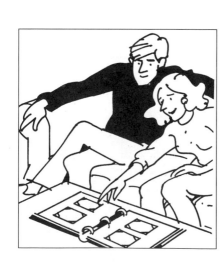

PAIRWORK. Now look at page 45. Make new conversations with a partner.

Asking about Family

4. Learn the new words. Look at the pictures and repeat the words after your teacher.

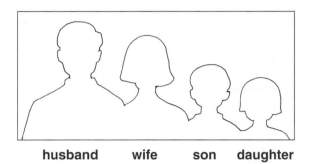

husband   wife   son   daughter

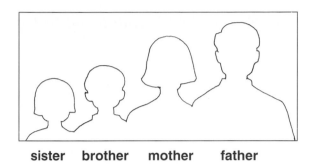

sister   brother   mother   father

Listen to the conversation and practice it with your teacher.

Maria: Hi, John. How are you?
John: Fine. How about you?
Maria: Pretty good. How's your sister?
John: Not so good.
Maria: Oh? What's wrong?
John: She's sad about her divorce.
Maria: Sad? That's too bad.

5. John is talking with Maria about his family. Listen to the conversations and draw a line from the person to the correct feeling.

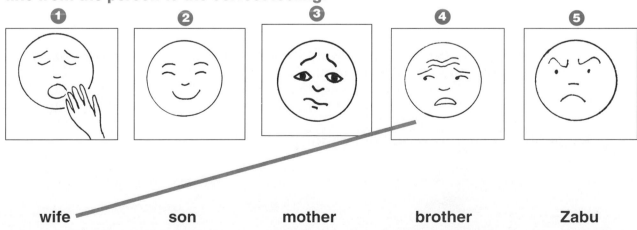

wife   son   mother   brother   Zabu

Asking about Family

6. Listen to the conversations and write the missing words. Then practice the conversations with a partner.

1. **Maria:** How's your daughter?

   John: She's _____.

   Maria: That's _____.

2. **Maria:** _____ _____ wife?

   John: Not so good.

   Maria: Oh? _____ _____?

   John: She's worried about work.

   Maria: Worried? That's _____

   _____ .

7. Write sentences about your family with the feelings on page 46.

Example: _My mother is worried._ _____

1. _____

2. _____

3. _____

4. _____

5. _____

6. _____

PAIRWORK. Ask your partner about his or her family. Then answer your partner's questions about your family.

Do people get divorced in your country?

What's Maria Doing Tomorrow?

1. Look at the pictures. Answer your teacher's questions. **(Teacher, see page 186.)**

Maria

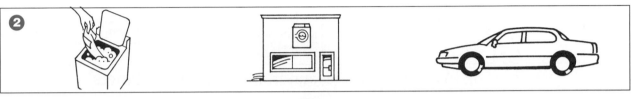

Stan

John

Zabu

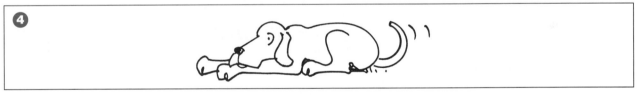

Tim and Kate

Mr. and Mrs. Morgan

Topic: common activities
Life skill: telephone skills
Structure: present continuous

Tomorrow's Activities

2. Learn the new words. Listen to the sentences. Repeat them after your teacher.

1. Maria is playing baseball in the park with her mother in the morning. She's taking the bus there.

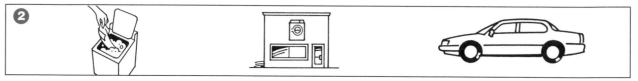

2. Stan is doing his laundry at the laundromat. He's driving there.

3. John is fixing his car in the garage with his father in the afternoon.

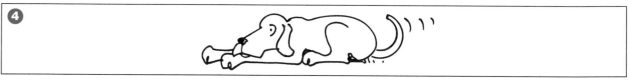

4. Zabu isn't doing anything.

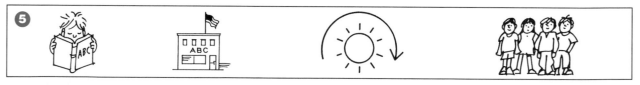

5. Tim and Kate are studying at school all day with their classmates.

6. Mr. and Mrs. Morgan are going fishing at the beach with their dog. They're walking there.

PAIRWORK. Now look at page 49. Make sentences with a partner.

Conversation

Wh_____	is he is she are they	_____ing?

3. Practice the conversations with your teacher.

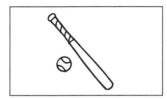

A: What is Maria doing tomorrow?
B: Playing baseball.

A: Where is she playing baseball?
B: In the park.

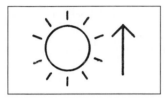

A: When is she playing baseball?
B: In the morning.

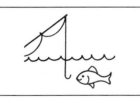

A: What are Mr. and Mrs. Morgan doing?
B: Fishing.

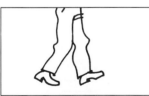

A: How are they **get**ting to the beach?
B: They're walking.

A: Who are they going there **with**?
B: Their dog.

PAIRWORK. Now look at page 49. Make conversations with a partner.

Sometimes we use **–ing** to talk about the future.	

Are you _____ ing tomorrow?	Yes, I am. No, I'm not.

I'm = I am

4. Practice the questions and answers with your teacher.

A: Are you coming to class tomorrow?
B: Yes, I am.

A: Are you working this Saturday?
B: No, I'm not.

A: Are you going shopping this weekend?
B: **I'm not sure.** Maybe.

PAIRWORK. Now ask and answer questions with a partner. You can ask about:

    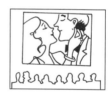

Writing Practice

5. Write sentences about yourself.

Examples: _I'm eating dinner after class today._

I'm not working this weekend.

1. _____

2. _____

3. _____

4. _____

Learn about Your Classmates

| Wh _____ are you _____-ing . . .? |

6. Practice the conversation with your teacher.

1. **A:** What are you doing next weekend?

   B: Going to the movies.

2. **A:** What movie are you going to?

   B: *The Lady with Green Hair.*

3. **A:** What day are you going?

   B: Sunday.

4. **A:** What time are you going?

   B: In the afternoon.

5. **A:** Who are you going with?

   B: My wife.

6. **A:** Where are you seeing the movie?

   B: Downtown.

7. **A:** How are you getting there?

   B: Walking.

PAIRWORK. Close your book. Ask a partner about next weekend or next summer.
Ask: 1. *What*   2. *What day*   3. *What time*   4. *Who*   5. *Where*   6. *How*

Write about your partner's plans:

Example: ___Ann is going to the park on Sunday._____

1. _____

2. _____

3. _____

4. _____

 Are there laundromats in your country?

On the Telephone

7. Listen to the four conversations. Number the places Maria is going.

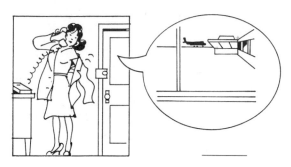

Listen again and number the people.

Mrs. Morgan	Stan	Nancy	Peter
_____	_____	_____	_____

8. PAIRWORK. Practice calling a partner on the telephone. Use the pictures next to the conversation.

A: Hello?

B: Hello. Is _____ there?

A: This is _____ speaking.

B: Oh hi, _____.
This is _____.

A: Hi, _____. Listen. I'm on my way out the door.

B: You are? Where are you going?

A: To _____ _____.

B: Oh. Well, have fun!

A: Thanks. Talk to you later!

B: OK. Goodbye.

UNIT 9

Is There a Post Office in Your Neighborhood?

1. Look at the pictures. Answer your teacher's questions. **(Teacher, see page 187.)**

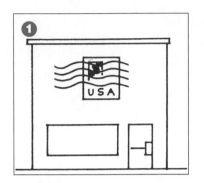

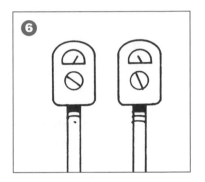

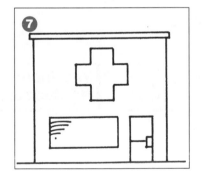

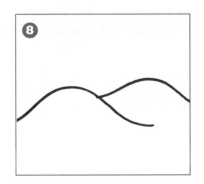

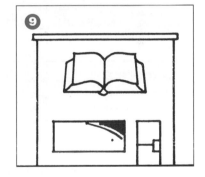

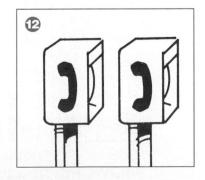

Topics: community resources
household items
Life skill: street directions
Structure: *there is/are*

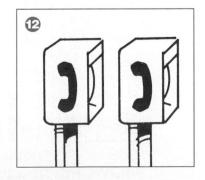 55

The Neighborhood

2. Learn the new words. Listen to the words. Repeat them after your teacher.

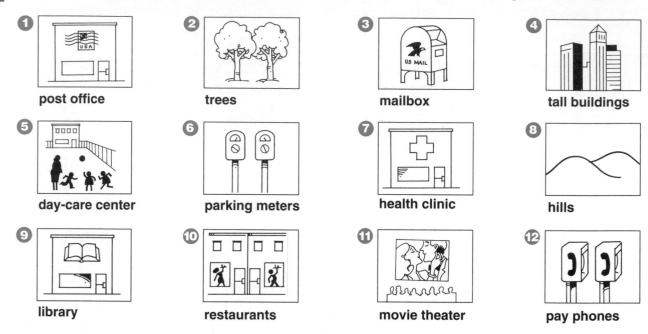

① post office	② trees	③ mailbox	④ tall buildings
⑤ day-care center	⑥ parking meters	⑦ health clinic	⑧ hills
⑨ library	⑩ restaurants	⑪ movie theater	⑫ pay phones

PAIRWORK. Practice with a partner. Student A, look at this page and say the words. Student B, look at page 55 and point to the pictures.

Learn about Your Classmates

| **Is** there a _____ ? | Yes, there is.
No, there isn't. | | **Are** there any_____? | Yes, there are.
No, there aren't. |

3. Practice the conversations with your teacher.

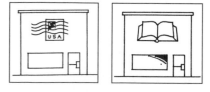

A: Is there a post office in your neighborhood?
B: Yes, there is.

A: Is there a library in your neighborhood?
B: No, there isn't.

A: Are there any restaurants in your neighborhood?
B: Yes, there are.

A: Are there any tall buildings in your neighborhood?
B: No, there aren't.

PAIRWORK. Now look at page 55 and ask a partner about his or her neighborhood.

4. Look at the pictures. Answer your teacher's questions. **(Teacher, see page 188.)**

In the House

5. Learn the new words. Listen to the words. Repeat them after your teacher.

1 TV

2 VCR

3 plants

4 dishwasher

5 pictures

6 basement

7 stairs

8 garage

9 bookshelves

10 ghost

11 closets

12 mice

PAIRWORK. Practice with a partner. Student A, look at this page and say the words. Student B, look at page 57 and point to the pictures.

Learn about Your Classmates

There's a		
There isn't a		
There are	some	_____ in _____.
	three	
	no	
There aren't	any	

6. Practice the sentences with your teacher.

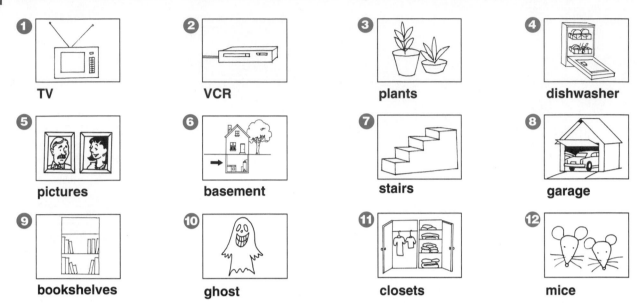

1. There's a basement in my house.

2. There isn't a dishwasher in my house.

3. There are $\left|\begin{array}{c}\text{some}\\\text{two}\end{array}\right|$ closets in my house.

4. There aren't any stairs in my house. *or* There are no stairs in my house.

PAIRWORK. Now look at page 57 and tell a partner about your house.

Listening Practice

7. Do you **remember** these places and things? Listen to your teacher and point to the correct picture.

① 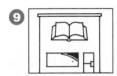 **②** 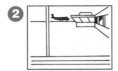 **③**  **④**

⑤ 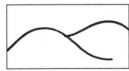 **⑥**  **⑦**  **⑧**

⑨  **⑩** 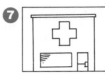 **⑪**  **⑫**

Learn about Your Classmates

8. Practice the conversations with your teacher.

A: Is there a zoo in your **hometown**?
B: Yes, there is.   *or*   No, there isn't.

A: Are there any hills in your hometown?
B: Yes, there are.   *or*   No, there aren't.

PAIRWORK. Now look at the pictures above. Ask a partner about his or her hometown. Write about your partner's hometown.

Example: There's an airport in Tony's hometown.

1. _____

2. _____

3. _____

4. _____

 Are health clinics in your country free?

Directions

9. Learn the new words. Repeat the words after your teacher. Then practice the conversation.

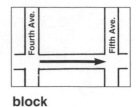

block

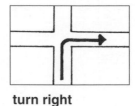

turn right

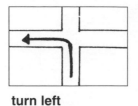

turn left

A: Excuse me. Is there a post office around here?

B: Yes, there is. Go three blocks and turn right.

A: Three blocks and turn right. Thank you.

10. Look at the pictures. Listen to the conversations and check (✔) the correct boxes.

	Blocks					Turn	
	1	2	3	4	5	right	left
1.			✔				✔
2.							
3.							
4.							
5.							

Write the places on the lines.

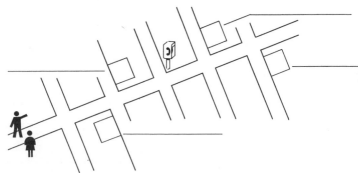

Directions

INFORMATION GAP. Work with a partner. Student A, look at this page. Student B, look at page 62.

11. Look at the map below and practice the conversation with your partner.

A: Excuse me. Is there a mailbox around here?
B: Yes, there is. Go two blocks and turn left.
A: Two blocks and turn left. Thank you.

Look at the pictures. Ask Student B about the missing places and draw a line to the correct location on the map. Then answer Student B's questions.

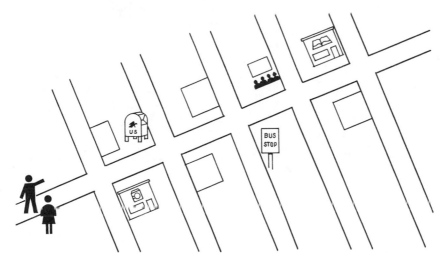

12. Write directions.

1. mailbox   <u>Go two blocks and turn left.</u>

2. pay phone   _____

3. day-care center   _____

4. park   _____

5. hospital   _____

INFORMATION GAP. Work with a partner. Student B, look at this page. Student A, look at page 61.

11. Look at the map below and practice the conversation with your partner.

A: Excuse me. Is there a mailbox around here?
B: Yes, there is. Go two blocks and turn left.
A: Two blocks and turn left. Thank you.

Look at the pictures. Answer Student A's questions. Then ask Student A about the missing places and draw a line to the correct location on the map.

12. Write directions.

1. mailbox   *Go two blocks and turn left.* _____

2. library _____

3. movie theater _____

4. laundromat _____

5. bus stop _____

Where's the Bedroom?

1. Look at the pictures. Answer your teacher's questions. **(Teacher, see page 188.)**

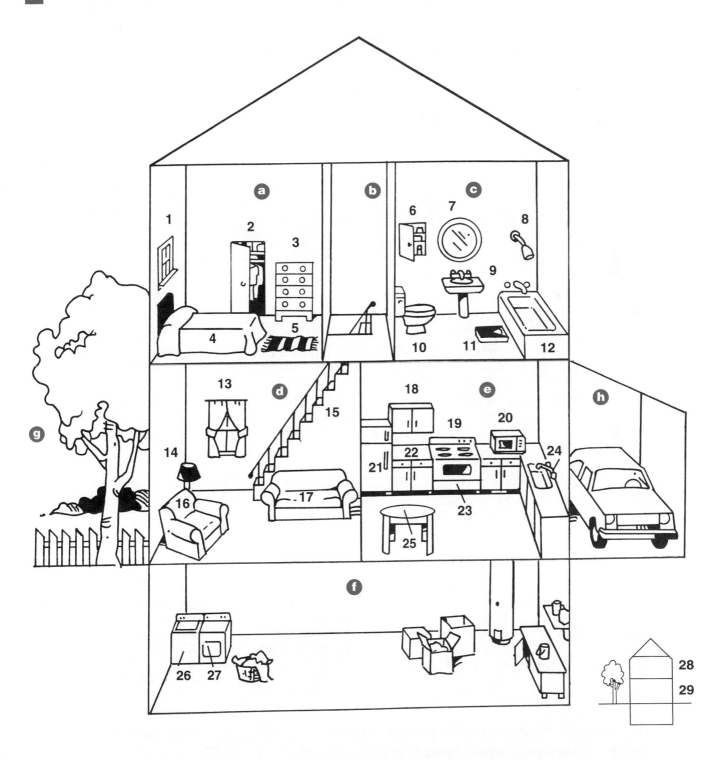

Topic: rooms and furnishings
Life skill: rental inquiries
Structure: *there is/are*

63

Rooms and Furniture

2. Learn the new words. Listen to the words. Repeat them after your teacher.

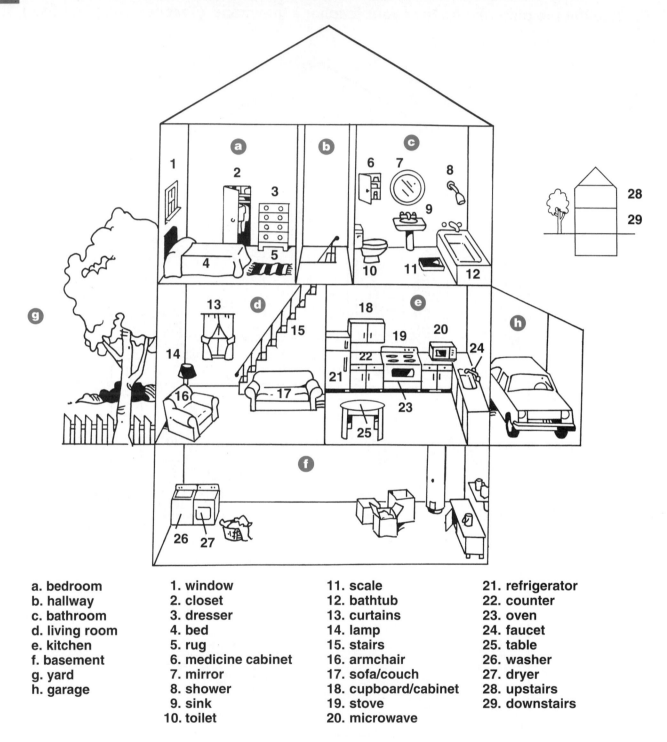

a. bedroom	1. window	11. scale	21. refrigerator
b. hallway	2. closet	12. bathtub	22. counter
c. bathroom	3. dresser	13. curtains	23. oven
d. living room	4. bed	14. lamp	24. faucet
e. kitchen	5. rug	15. stairs	25. table
f. basement	6. medicine cabinet	16. armchair	26. washer
g. yard	7. mirror	17. sofa/couch	27. dryer
h. garage	8. shower	18. cupboard/cabinet	28. upstairs
	9. sink	19. stove	29. downstairs
	10. toilet	20. microwave	

PAIRWORK. Practice with a partner. Student A, look at this page and say the words. Student B, look at page 63 and point to the pictures.

Where's My Watch?

3. Listen to John and May. Draw a line from the picture to the correct location.

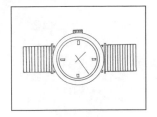   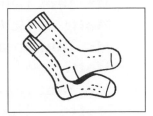

4. Write sentences.

1. ___The watch is_____

2. _____

3. _____

4. _____

Conversation

5. Listen to the telephone conversation. Then practice it with a partner.

Mr. Tan: Hello?
Matt: Hello. Is Mr. Tan there?
Mr. Tan: Speaking.
Matt: Mr. Tan, I'm looking for a house.
Mr. Tan: How many bedrooms?
Matt: Three.
Mr. Tan: There's a three-bedroom house on Green Street.
Matt: Are there closets in all the bedrooms?
Mr. Tan: Yes, there are.
Matt: Is there a yard?
Mr. Tan: No, there isn't. Any other questions?
Matt: No. But thank you for the information.
Mr. Tan: You're welcome. Goodbye.

Houses For Rent
Furnished
Call Mr. Tan
555-9811

Listen and Write

6. Listen to the telephone conversation and write the missing words. Then practice it with your partner.

Manager: Hello.
Nancy: Hello. Is the manager there?
Manager: Speaking.
Nancy: I'm _____ for an apartment.
Manager: How many bedrooms?
Nancy: _____ .
Manager: There's a _____ –bedroom apartment on Polk Street.
Nancy: Is there a _____ _____ _____?
Manager: Yes, there is.
Nancy: Are there many _____ in the kitchen?
Manager: No, there aren't. Any other questions?
Nancy: No. But _____ _____ for the information.
Manager: You're welcome. Goodbye.

Apts. For Rent
Unfurnished
Call Manager
555-8554

Do most people in your country live in apartments or houses?

In the House

INFORMATION GAP. Work with a partner. Student A, look at this page. Student B, look at page 68.

7. Practice the conversation with your partner.

A: Where's the refrigerator?
B: It's in the kitchen next to the sink.

A: Where's the little table?
B: It's in the bedroom beside the bed.

Look at the house below. Ask Student B where these things are, and draw a line to the right place in the picture. Then answer Student B's questions.

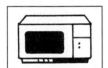  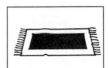

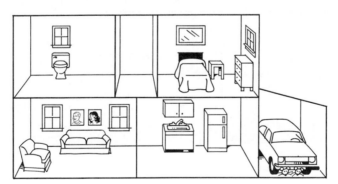

Now write sentences about the locations.

Example: ___The microwave is on top of the refrigerator.___

1. _____

2. _____

3. _____

4. _____

INFORMATION GAP. Work with a partner. Student B, look at this page. Student A, look at page 67.

7. Practice the conversation with your partner.

A: Where's the refrigerator?
B: It's in the kitchen next to the sink.

A: Where's the little table?
B: It's in the bedroom beside the bed.

Look at the house below. Answer Student A's questions. Then ask Student A where these things are and draw a line to the right place in the picture.

    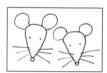

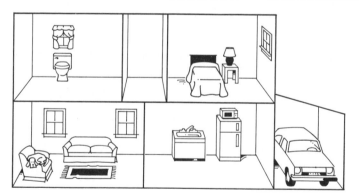

Now write sentences about the locations.

Example: _____ The dresser is under the bedroom window. _____

1. _____

2. _____

3. _____

4. _____

UNIT 11

What Time Is It, Please?

Look at the clocks. Repeat the times after your teacher.

1

10:00
It's ten o'clock.

2

7:30
It's seven thirty.
It's half past seven.

3

11:15
It's eleven fifteen.
It's a quarter after eleven.

4

4:45
It's four forty-five.
It's a quarter to five.

5

12:00
It's noon.
It's midnight.

Topic: daily routine
Life skill: telling time
    relating personal problems
Structure: present tense

69

2. Listen and number the pictures.

a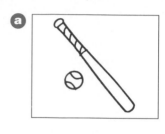
_____

b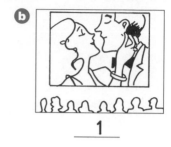
1

c
_____

d
_____

e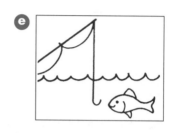
_____

f
_____

Listen again and number the clocks.

a
_____

b
_____

c
1

d
_____

e
_____

f
_____

3. Listen. Draw the hands on the clocks.

1
2
3
4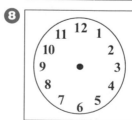

5
6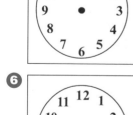
7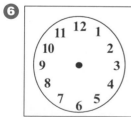
8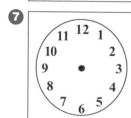

When Do You Get Up?

4. Look at the pictures. Answer your teacher's questions. (Teacher, see page 189.)

Your Daily Routine

5. Learn the new words. Listen to the words. Repeat them after your teacher.

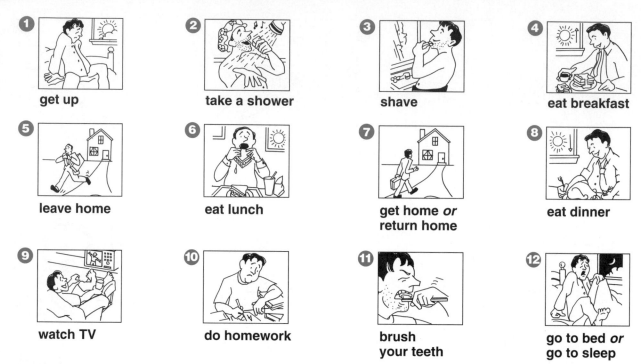

1. get up
2. take a shower
3. shave
4. eat breakfast
5. leave home
6. eat lunch
7. get home *or* return home
8. eat dinner
9. watch TV
10. do homework
11. brush your teeth
12. go to bed *or* go to sleep

PAIRWORK. Practice with a partner. Student A, look at this page and say the words. Student B, look at page 71 and point to the pictures.

Listen and Write

6. Listen to Stan and complete the sentences.

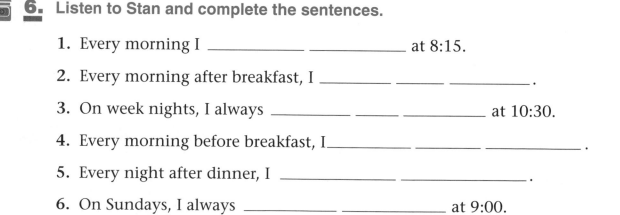

1. Every morning I _____ _____ at 8:15.

2. Every morning after breakfast, I _____ _____ _____.

3. On week nights, I always _____ _____ _____ at 10:30.

4. Every morning before breakfast, I_____ _____ _____.

5. Every night after dinner, I _____ _____.

6. On Sundays, I always _____ _____ at 9:00.

7. I always _____ _____ at noon.

8. Every morning I _____ _____ at 7:00.

RIGHT NOW *or* FUTURE -ing	USUALLY *or* EVERY DAY **do** -i̶n̶g̶
Examples: 1. What are you eat**ing** now? 2. When are you go**ing** to bed tonight?	Examples: 1. What **do** you usually eat for breakfast? 2. When **do** you go to bed every night?

Learn about Your Classmates

> **When do you** _____?

7. Practice the conversations with your teacher.

A: When do you get up?
B: At 6:30.

A: When do you get home?
B: **About** 5:30.

A: When do you brush your teeth?
B: Before breakfast.

A: When do you take a shower?
B: After work.

A: When do you watch TV?
B: In the evening.

A: When do you shave?
B: I don't shave.

> **don't = do not**

PAIRWORK. Now look at page 71. Ask a partner about his or her daily routine.

Talking about Problems

8. Do you remember these feelings? Cover the words. Listen to your teacher and point to the correct picture.

①	②	③	④	⑤	⑥
confused	scared	worried	angry	tired	sad

9. Listen to the conversations and write the missing words. Then practice the conversations with a partner.

1. **Tom:** Hi, Ann.

   Ann: Hi, Tom. Hey. Is something wrong?
   Are you _____?

   Tom: I'm very tired. I work too much.

   Ann: When do you _____ for work?

   Tom: _____ _____.

   Ann: When do you get home?

   Tom: _____ _____.

   Ann: Oh no. That's **terrible!**

2. **Sue:** Hi, Tony.

   Tony: Hi, Sue. Hey. Is something wrong?
   Are you _____?

   Sue: I'm very worried. I study hard but
   I don't understand my homework.

   Tony: When do you do your _____?

   Sue: I start _____ _____.

   Tony: When do you finish?

   Sue: Sometimes _____ _____.

   Tony: Oh no. That's terrible!

   PAIRWORK. Look at the pictures at the top of the page. Make new conversations with your partner.

Do people in your country talk about problems with friends?

Do You Work on Sundays?

1. Look at the pictures. Answer your teacher's questions. **(Teacher, see page 189.)**

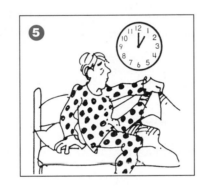

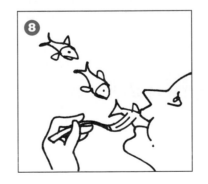

Topic: habitual activities
Life skill: talking about work
Structure: present tense

abits

2. Learn the new words. Listen to the words. Repeat them after your teacher.

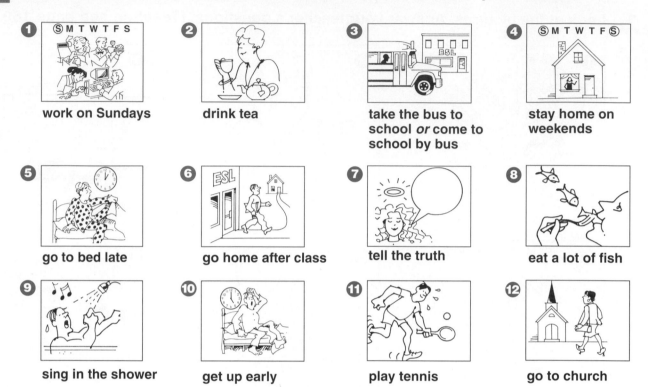

1 work on Sundays

2 drink tea

3 take the bus to school *or* come to school by bus

4 stay home on weekends

5 go to bed late

6 go home after class

7 tell the truth

8 eat a lot of fish

9 sing in the shower

10 get up early

11 play tennis

12 go to church

PAIRWORK. Practice with a partner. Student A, look at this page and say the words. Student B, look at page 75 and point to the pictures.

isten and Write

3. Listen to May and complete the sentences.

1. On Fridays and Saturdays, I ___*go to bed*___ late.

2. I _____ every morning.

3. Sometimes I _____ on Sundays.

4. Sometimes I _____ on Sundays.

5. I _____ to school by bus every day.

6. I _____ every Saturday.

7. On weekdays, I _____ early.

8. I usually _____ on weekends.

Learn about Your Classmates

Do you _____?	Yes, I do.
	No, I don't.

4. Practice the conversations with your teacher.

A: Do you drink tea?
B: Yes, I do.

A: Do you get up early?
B: No, I don't.

PAIRWORK. Now look at page 75. Ask and answer questions with a partner.

Do you have . . . ?

5. Look at the pictures below. Answer your teacher's questions. For example:

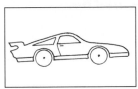

A: Do you have a car?
B: Yes, I do. *or* No, I don't.

a car

❶

a bicycle

❷

a dog

❸

children

❹

American friends

❺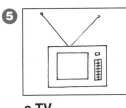

a TV

❻

a microwave

❼

red socks

❽

PAIRWORK. Now ask and answer questions with a partner.

Conversation

I	work don't work	on Sundays.

6. Practice the conversations with your teacher.

A: I get up early. What about you?
B: I don't get up early.

A: I take the bus to school. What about you?
B: Me too.

A: I don't drink tea. What about you?
B: Me neither.

PAIRWORK. Now look at page 75. Make new conversations with a partner.

7. Write sentences about your habits.

1. I _____

2. _____

3. _____

4. _____

5. _____

Talking about Work

 8. Learn the new words. Listen to the words. Repeat them after your teacher.
Then listen to Tony talk about his job.

full-time job   part-time job   lunch break   hours   boss

I have a full-time job. I work 6 hours a day 5 days a week. I don't have bad hours. I have
good hours. I work 3 hours in the morning. Then I have a lunch break. I work 3 more
hours in the afternoon. I have a good boss, so I'm happy with my job. I work Monday to
Friday. I stay home on weekends.

Listening Practice

9. Listen to Sue, Lee, and Maria talk about their jobs. Check *yes* or *no* in the
boxes below.

	SUE		LEE		MARIA	
	yes	no	yes	no	yes	no
full-time job	✔					
part-time job		✔				
good hours						
lunch break						
good boss						
work on weekends						

10. Practice the conversations with your teacher.

A: Do you have a full-time job?
B: No, I don't.

A: Do you have a part-time job?
B: Yes, I do.

Ask four classmates about their jobs. Write *yes* or *no* in the boxes below.

Classmate's name				
Full-time job				
Part-time job				
Good hours				
Lunch break				
Good boss				

Writing Practice

11. Write sentences about your job. Use *have* or *don't have*.

1. _____

2. _____

3. _____

4. _____

5. _____

 Do people in your country work on weekends?

UNIT 13 — How Do You Get to Work?

1. Look at the pictures. Answer your teacher's questions. **(Teacher, see page 189.)**

How?

What time?

What kind?

Who/with?

How long?

How many?

What day?

What/do?

Where?

Topic: habitual activities
Life skill: public transportation
Structure: present tense

81

Asking about Habits

2. Learn the new words. Listen to the questions. Repeat them after your teacher.

1. **How** do you | **get** | to work?
                  | go |

2. **What time** do you start work?
   When

3. **What kind** of clothes do you wear at work?

4. **Who** do you eat lunch **with**?

5. **How long** do you work every day?

6. **How many** days do you work every week?

7. **What day** do you have off?

8. **What** do you do on your day off?

9. **Where** do you go on vacation?

PAIRWORK. Practice with a partner. Student A, look at this page and ask the questions. Student B, look at page 81 and point to the pictures.

Telling about Habits

3. Repeat the answers after your teacher.

How?

What time?

What kind?

Who/with?

How long?

1. I **usually** walk.
   I take the bus.
   (By bus.)

2. **Sometimes** at 8:00
   and **sometimes** at
   8:30.

3. I wear work clothes.
   I wear casual clothes.
   I dress up.

4. I **always** eat with my
   coworkers.
   Nobody. I eat alone.

5. I work (for) eight hours
   a day.

6. I work five days a week.
   It depends. Sometimes five
   and sometimes six.

7. I have Saturday and Sunday off.

8. I relax at home.
   I go to the movies.

9. I usually visit my sister.
   I **never** have vacations. *or*
   I don't have vacations.

How many?

What day?

What/do?

Where?

4. PAIRWORK. Look at page 81. Ask and answer questions with a partner.

Conversation

What do you do on _____?

 5. **Listen to the conversation between Maria and her neighbor. Then say it with your teacher.**

A: What do you usually do on Sundays?
B: In the morning I go to church.

A: Who do you go with?
B: My sister.

A: What do you do after church?
B: Sometimes I go to the park with my boyfriend, Stan.

A: How do you get there?
B: We usually take the bus.

A: What do you do for your summer vacation?
B: I like to relax and read books.

A: What kind of books do you read?
B: I always read love stories.

A: What do you do in the evening after work?
B: I don't do anything.

PAIRWORK. Now close your book and ask a partner what he or she does on Sundays, on weekends, after work, and on vacation. Ask:

What/do?
Where?
How long?
Who/with?
What time?

Transportation

6. Learn the new words. Look at the pictures. Repeat the words after your teacher.

get on

get off

fare

Listen to Maria's telephone conversation. Then practice it with your teacher.

Bus Office: City Bus. Can I help you?
Maria: Yes. I'm at the airport. I'm going downtown. What bus do I take?
Bus Office: Take the #19.
Maria: Where do I get on?
Bus Office: At Main and 32nd.
Maria: Where do I get off?
Bus Office: At 4th Street.
Maria: How much is the fare?
Bus Office: $1.00.
Maria: Thank you.
Bus Office: You're welcome. Goodbye.

7. Listen to the telephone conversations. Write the missing information.

	number	get on		get off		fare
1.	7	Polk and	2nd		42nd	80¢
2.		Post and				
3.		Holly and				
4.		Oak and				

Transportation

8. Write questions to complete the conversation. Then practice it with a partner.

Bus Office: City Bus. Can I help you?
Caller: Yes. I'm going to the subway. I'm at General Hospital.

_____?

Bus Office: Take the #33.

Caller: _____?

Bus Office: At 12th and Broadway.

Caller: _____?

Bus Office: At Pacific.

Caller: _____?

Bus Office: 75 cents.
Caller: Thank you.

Bus Office: You're welcome. Goodbye.

9. PAIRWORK. Look at the pictures. Tell your partner where you go on the bus.

What number?   Where?   Where?   How much?

Write sentences.

1. _____

2. _____

3. _____

4. _____

 In your country, how do most people travel: by bus, train, car, or bicycle?

UNIT 14
Where Do You Keep Your Money?

1. Look at the pictures. Answer your teacher's questions. **(Teacher, see page 190.)**

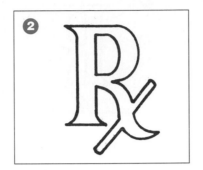

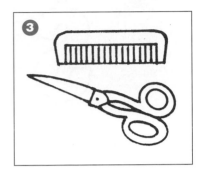

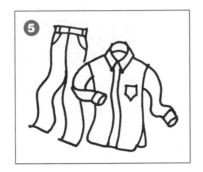

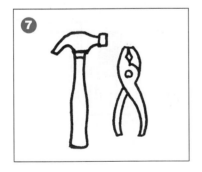

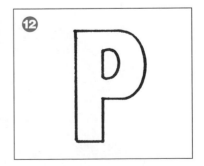

Topic: stores and merchandise
Life skills: banking
   inquiring about store hours
Structure: present tense

Stores

2. Learn the new words. Listen to the words. Repeat them after your teacher.

1 bank
keep your money

2 drug store
buy medicine

3 barber shop *or* hair salon
get a haircut

4 supermarket *or* grocery store
buy food

5 department store
buy clothes

6 second-hand store *or* thrift shop
buy used things

7 hardware store
buy tools

8 auto repair shop
fix your car

9 furniture store
buy chairs, beds, and other furniture

10 gas station
get gas

11 produce store
buy fruit and vegetables

12 parking lot
park your car

PAIRWORK. Practice with a partner. Student A, look at this page and say the words. Student B, look at page 87 and point to the pictures.

3. Practice the conversations with your teacher.

A: Where do you keep your money?
B: At First Bank.
A: How far is it from your house?
B: About a five-minute walk.

A: Where do you buy medicine?
B: At Super Drugs.
A: How far is it from your house?
B: About three blocks.

A: Where do you buy food?
B: At Lo-Cost Market.
A: How far is it from your house?
B: Ten minutes by bus.

How far?
A ten-minute walk.
A five-minute drive.
Fifteen minutes by bus.
Three blocks.

PAIRWORK. Now look at page 87. Make new conversations with a partner.
Ask:
1. Where?
2. How far?

Banking

4. Listen to the conversation and practice it with your teacher.

Teller: Can I help you?
John: Yes. Can you please **cash this check**?
Teller: Do you have an **account** with our bank?
John: Yes, I do.
Teller: All right. Please sign your name on the back of the check.
John: OK. And how much money do I have in my account?
Teller: You have $480.00.
John: Thank you.

5. Listen to the conversations. Circle *yes* or *no* and write how much is in the account.

	Account?	How much?
Conversation 1:	yes no	$ _____
Conversation 2:	yes no	$ _____
Conversation 3:	yes no	$ _____
Conversation 4:	yes no	$ _____
Conversation 5:	yes no	$ _____

 Do most people in your country have a bank account?

Do You Have the Time, Please?

6. Look at the clocks. Repeat the times after your teacher.

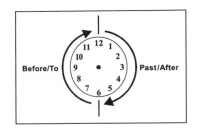

It's seven twenty.
It's twenty **after** seven.
It's twenty **past** seven.

It's two thirty-five
It's twenty-five **to** three.
It's twenty-five **before** three.

7. Listen. Draw the hands on the clocks.

① ② ③

④ ⑤ ⑥

⑦ ⑧

Opening and Closing Times

8. Repeat the names of the places after your teacher. Then listen and write the opening and closing times in the boxes below.

1

Public Library

	open	close
Today		
Saturday		
Sunday		

2

Lane's Department Store

	open	close
Today		
Saturday		
Sunday		

3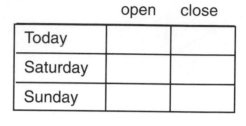

First National Bank

	open	close
Today		
Saturday		
Sunday		

4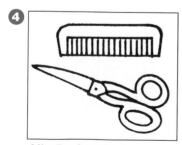

Al's Barber Shop

	open	close
Today		
Saturday		
Sunday		

UNIT 15

Where's the Supermarket?

1. Look at the pictures. Answer your teacher's questions. **(Teacher, see page 190.)**

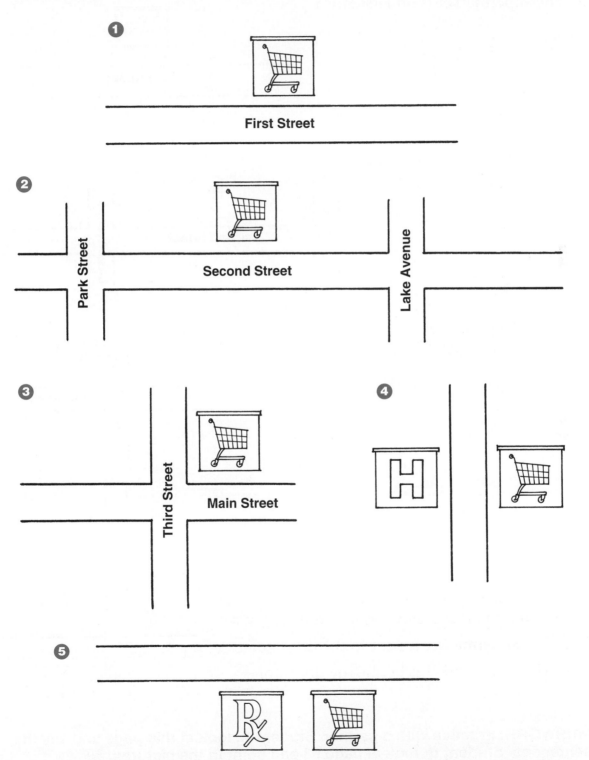

❶

First Street

❷

Park Street

Second Street

Lake Avenue

❸

Third Street

Main Street

❹

❺

Topic: street locations
Life skill: grocery shopping
Structure: *there is/are*

93

Street Locations

2. Learn the new words. Listen to the sentences. Repeat them after your teacher.

1. The supermarket is on First Street.

First Street

2. The supermarket is on Second Street between Park Street and Lake Avenue. It's in the middle of the block.

3. The supermarket is on the corner of Third and Main.

   or It's on Third at the corner of Main.

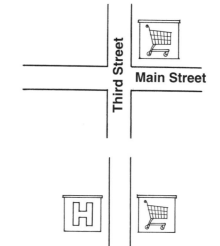

4. The supermarket is across from the hospital.

5. The supermarket is next door to the drug store.

   or The supermarket is next to the drug store.

   or The supermarket is beside the drug store.

PAIRWORK. Practice with a partner. Student A, look at this page and say the sentences. Student B, look at page 93 and point to the pictures.

3. Look at the map. Your teacher will ask where the stores are. Listen and answer.

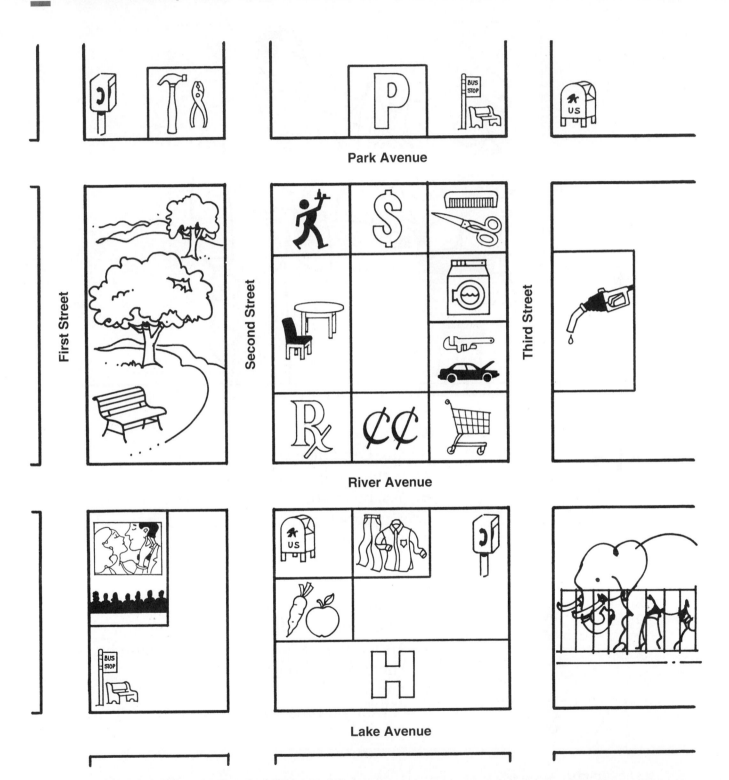

Park Avenue

First Street

Second Street

Third Street

River Avenue

Lake Avenue

4. Listen to the conversation. Then practice it with your teacher.

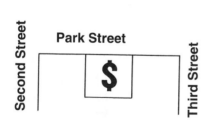

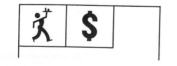

A: Excuse me.

B: Yes. Can I help you?

A: Is there a drug store around here?

B: Yes, there's one at the corner of Second and River.

A: Thanks a lot.

B: You're welcome.

A: **Also**, is there a bank around here?

B: Yes, there's one on Park between Second and Third.

A: Thanks.

B: **Don't mention it.**

A: Also, is there a good restaurant around here?

B: There's one next door to the bank.

A: And . . .

B: I'm sorry. **I have to go now!**

A: OK. Thanks. Bye.

PAIRWORK. Now look at page 95. Make new conversations with a partner.

Grocery Shopping

INFORMATION GAP. Work with a partner. Student A, look at this page. Student B, look at page 98.

5. Learn the new words. Listen to the words. Repeat them after your teacher.

pound = lb.   **dozen = doz.**   **quart = qt.**   **each = ea.**

6. Repeat the names of the foods after your teacher. Then practice the conversations with a partner.

1. **A:** How much is coffee?
   B: $5.95 a pound.

2. **A:** How much are lemons?
   B: 10¢ each.

Ask Student B about the missing prices and write them on the lines. Then answer Student B's questions.

Coffee: **$5.95 /lb.**

Lemons: **10¢ ea.**

Potatoes: **39¢ /lb.**

Orange juice: _____

Cookies: _____

Melons: **50¢ ea.**

Milk: **69¢ /qt.**

Eggs: **$1.00 /doz.**

Onions: _____

Apples: _____

7. Write sentences.

1. coffee   _Coffee is $5.95 a pound._

2. orange juice   _____

3. cookies   _____

4. onions   _____

5. apples   _____

 Is food more expensive in the United States or in your country?

Grocery Shopping

INFORMATION GAP. Work with a partner. Student B, look at this page. Student A, look at page 97.

5. Learn the new words. Listen to the words. Repeat them after your teacher.

pound = lb.   **dozen = doz.**   **quart = qt.**   **each = ea.**

6. Repeat the names of the foods after your teacher. Then practice the conversations with a partner.

1. **A:** How much is coffee?
   B: $5.95 a pound.

2. **A:** How much are lemons?
   B: 10¢ each.

Answer Student A's questions. Then ask Student A about the missing prices and write them on the lines.

Coffee: **$5.95 /lb.**

Lemons: **10¢ ea.**

Potatoes: _____

Orange juice: **$1.75 /qt.**

Cookies: **2.50 /doz.**

Melons: _____

Milk: _____

Eggs: _____

Onions: **39¢/lb.**

Apples: **25¢ ea.**

7. Write sentences.

1. coffee _____Coffee is $5.95 a pound._____

2. potatoes _____

3. melons _____

4. milk _____

5. eggs _____

 Is food more expensive in the United States or in your country?

UNIT 16

What Time Does May Leave Home?

1. Look at the pictures. Answer your teacher's questions. **(Teacher, see page 190.)**

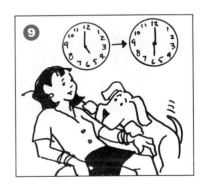

Topic: daily routine
Life skill: filling out a schedule
Structure: present tense

May's Daily Schedule

2. Learn the new words. Listen to the words. Repeat them after your teacher.

1 leave home	**2** catch the bus
3 get to work	**4** start work *or* begin work
5 take a coffee break	**6** eat lunch
7 finish work *or* get off work	**8** get home
9 relax	**10** cook dinner
11 read the paper	**12** watch TV

PAIRWORK. Practice with a partner. Student A, look at this page and say the words. Student B, look at page 99 and point to the pictures.

Listen and Write

3. Listen to May and complete the sentences.

1. Most mornings I ___get to work___ at about 8:00.

2. Most days I _____ after work.

3. Every day I _____ _____ at 8:00.

4. Most nights I _____ _____ before I go to sleep.

5. I always _____ _____ _____ in front of my house.

6. Most evenings I _____ _____ _____ after dinner.

7. Every morning I _____ _____ _____ _____ at work.

8. Every day I _____ _____ at 4:30.

Conversation

I you we they $\}$ **do**	he she it $\}$ **does**
What time do you start work? **Where do they live?**	**What time does she start work?** **Where does he live?**

4. Practice the conversations with your teacher.

A: What time does May leave home in the morning?
B: At 7:25.
A: What time do you leave home?
B: About eight o'clock.

A: What time does May eat lunch every day?
B: From twelve to half past twelve.
A: What time do you eat lunch?
B: From twelve-thirty **until** one o'clock.

A: What time does May cook dinner?
B: At six.
A: What time do you cook dinner?
B: I don't cook dinner!

PAIRWORK. Now look at page 99. Make new conversations with a partner.
First ask about May. Then ask about your partner.

Does	he she it	_____ ?	Yes,	he she it	does.
			No,	he she it	doesn't.

5. Practice the conversations with your teacher.

A: Do you have a brother?
B: Yes, I do.
A: Does he get up early?
B: Yes, he does.

A: Do you have a daughter?
B: Yes, I do.
A: Does she drink tea?
B: No, she doesn't.

A: Do you have a sister?
B: No, I don't.

PAIRWORK. Now look at page 75. Ask a partner about people in his or her family.

Writing Practice

6. Read the questions and then write the answers.

Example: Does your teacher speak English? _____ *Yes, he does.* _____

1. Does your school have many students? _____

2. Does your teacher have long hair? _____

3. Does your classroom have a big chalkboard? _____

4. Does the classmate to your left speak your language? _____

5. Does this **textbook** have many pictures? _____

6. Does the classmate to your right wear **glasses**? _____

I You We They	**play** tennis. **don't play** tennis.	He She	**plays** tennis. **doesn't play** tennis.

Irregular words			
I You We They	**have** children. **go** to sleep late.	He She	**has** children. **goes** to sleep late.

7. Practice the conversations with your teacher.

A: My husband plays tennis. What about your husband?
B: My husband plays tennis, **too.**

A: My son doesn't get up early. How about your son?
B: My son doesn't get up early, **either.**

A: My sister works on Sundays. What about your sister?
B: I don't have a sister.

PAIRWORK. Now look at page 75. Make new conversations with a partner.

Writing Practice

8. Write about your family or your partner's family.

Examples: _____My sister eats a lot of fish._____

_____Juan's brother doesn't play baseball._____

1. _____

2. _____

3. _____

Maria's Weekly Schedule

9. Listen to Maria talk about her weekly schedule. Write the missing information.

	Weekdays	Saturdays	Sundays
8:00	work		
9:00		go to the bank and go shopping	
10:00			_____
11:00			
12:00	_____		eat lunch
1:00	work		do laundry
2:00		_____	
3:00			_____
4:00			
5:00			
6:00	_____		eat dinner
7:00	read the paper and watch TV	_____	_____
8:00			
9:00			
10:00			

Do people hurry more in your country or in the United States?

How Often Do You Go Dancing?

1. Look at the pictures. Answer your teacher's questions. **(Teacher, see page 191.)**

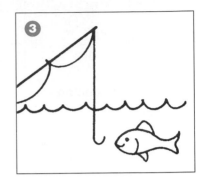

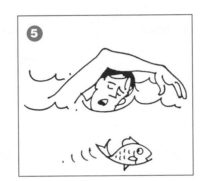

Topic: sports and leisure activities
Life skill: describing interests
Structure: expressions of frequency

Leisure Activities

2. Learn the new words. Listen to the words. Repeat them after your teacher.

1 go dancing	2 play cards	3 go fishing	4 watch a movie
5 go swimming	6 exercise	7 eat out	8 take a nap
9 take a vacation	10 go bowling	11 go to church	12 kiss your husband/wife

PAIRWORK. Practice with a partner. Student A, look at this page and say the words. Student B, look at page 105 and point to the pictures.

Listen and Write

3. Listen and complete the sentences.

1. I always ___*go dancing*___ on Friday.

2. My sister usually _____ _____ on Sunday.

3. My wife and I never _____ _____ _____.

4. I sometimes _____ _____ in the summer.

5. My children usually _____ _____ _____ on Saturday.

6. I usually don't _____ _____ because it's expensive!

7. My parents sometimes _____ _____ on the weekend.

8. My family _____ _____ _____ on Sunday.

4. Listen to the questions and answers. Repeat them after your teacher. Study them at home.

How often do you _____?

1.

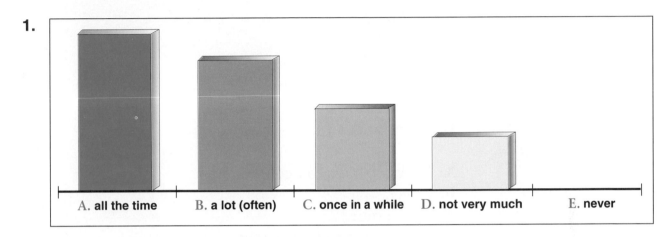

A. all the time   B. a lot (often)   C. once in a while   D. not very much   E. never

2.

every	day week night Sunday summer

3.

once a twice a three times a	week day year

4.

It depends.

Writing Practice

5. Read the questions. Write short answers.

Example: How often do you go to the movies? ____Every Saturday.____

1. How often do you go fishing? _____

2. How often do you eat out? _____

3. How often do you take a vacation? _____

4. How often do you go bowling? _____

5. How often do you go swimming? _____

6. How often do you play cards? _____

7. How often do you go to church? _____

8. How often do you take a nap? _____

Conversation

6. Practice the conversations with your teacher.

A: How often do you go dancing?
B: Every weekend.
A: Where do you go?
B: To Discoland.

A: How often do you play cards?
B: About once a month.
A: Who do you play with?
B: Friends from work.

A: How often do you go to church?
B: Never.
A: **How come?**
B: Because I'm not **Christian.**

PAIRWORK. Now look at page 105. Make new conversations with a partner.
Ask: 1. *How often?* 2. *Where?* or *Who/with?* or *When?* or *What kind?*

Writing Practice

7. Write about your partner's leisure activities.

Example: _____ Ann goes fishing every weekend. _____

1. _____

2. _____

3. _____

4. _____

5. _____

6. _____

Spelling

A. read → read**s**	B. relax → relax**es**	C. play play**s**
argue → argue**s**	watch → wat**ches**	↑___ vowel
	kiss → kiss**es**	study stud**ies**
	wash → wash**es**	↑___ consonant

8. Add *-s* or *-es* to these words.

1. swim _____
2. teach _____
3. write _____
4. fix _____
5. do _____

6. buy _____
7. dance _____
8. finish _____
9. study _____
10. stay _____

9. Look at the pictures and read about Maria's leisure activities. Write the missing words.

1.

2.

Maria has time for leisure activities at night and on the weekends. After work, she's usually tired. On weeknights, she _____ at home. She often _____ TV.
                          1.   2.
Every Friday after work, she _____ her clothes. But
                                          3.
Maria doesn't work on the weekends. She has fun then. On
Saturday, she _____ tennis with a friend. She
                        4.
often _____ dancing with her boyfriend, Stan.
              5.
Once in a while, she _____ with him. But most of
                                  6.
the time, she _____ him a lot!
                        7.

4.    5.    6.   7.

Sports and Leisure Activities

10. Learn the new words. Look at the pictures. Repeat the words after your teacher.

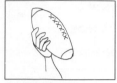   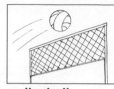

football   soccer   basketball   volleyball

Listen to Pablo, Sue, Jane, and Matt. Put a check (✔) above their sports and leisure activities.

1. Pablo

 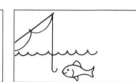

Every Saturday morning

2. Sue

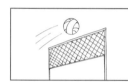   

3. Jane

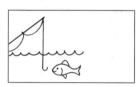   

4. Matt

 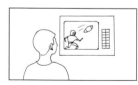 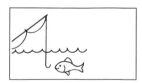

Listen again. Under the pictures, write how often.

 Do many people play sports in your country? Which sports are popular?

What Does Sue Do?

1. Look at the pictures. Answer your teacher's questions. **(Teacher, see page 191.)**

Topic: occupations and duties
Life skill: reporting emergencies
Structure: present tense

111

Jobs and Duties

2. Learn the new words. Listen to the words. Repeat them after your teacher.

1 police officer
keep the streets safe

2 fire fighter
put out fires

3 mail carrier
deliver the mail

4 bus driver
drive a bus

5 teacher
teach lessons

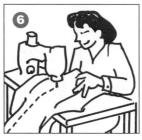

6 seamstress
sew clothes

7 housewife
take care of the house

8 cashier
take your money and give you change

9 secretary
work in an office

10 operator
help with phone calls

11 waitress/waiter
serve meals at a restaurant

12 dentist
take care of your teeth

13 janitor
clean buildings

14 security guard
watch stores

15 mechanic
fix cars

16 factory worker
work in a factory

PAIRWORK. Practice with a partner. Student A, look at this page and say the words. Student B, look at page 111 and point to the pictures.

Listen and Write

> A.M. = midnight to noon
> P.M. = noon to midnight

3. Listen. Write the number of each person under the correct picture.

_____ _____ _____

_____ _____ _____

_____   1   7:00 P.M.   _____

Listen again. Write the time each person starts work.
Remember to write A.M. or P.M.

Conversation

4. Practice the conversations with your teacher.

A: What's Joe's job?
B: He's a mail carrier.
A: What does he do every day?
B: He delivers the mail.

A: What's Sue's job?
B: She's a police officer.
A: What does she do every day?
B: She keeps the streets safe.

PAIRWORK. Now look at page 111. Make new conversations with a partner.

Police and Fire

5. Learn the new words. Look at the pictures. Repeat the words after your teacher.

1 fire station

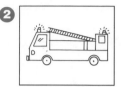
2 fire truck

3 police station

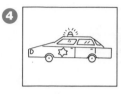
4 police car

6. Read about Tony and answer the questions.

Hi. My name is Tony Park. I'm a fire fighter. I work 12 hours a day 3 days a week. I work the **night shift.** I go to work at the fire station at 6:00 in the evening. I **get off** at 6:00 in the morning. At the fire station, I wait for calls from **911**. I drive a fire truck to homes and buildings. Then I put out fires.

1. What does Tony do? __He_____

2. What shift does he work? _____

3. Where does he go to work? _____

4. What does he drive? _____

Now read about Sue and answer the questions.

Hi. My name is Sue Sims. I'm a police officer. I work 8 hours a day 5 days a week. I work the **day shift**. I go to work at the police station at 7:00 in the morning. I get off work at 3:00 in the afternoon. With my partner, I drive a police car around the city. I watch out for **trouble** and I keep the streets safe.

1. What does Sue do? __She_____

2. What shift does she work? _____

3. Where does she go to work? _____

4. What does she drive? _____

911 Emergency

 7. Learn the new words. Look at the pictures. Repeat the words after your teacher.

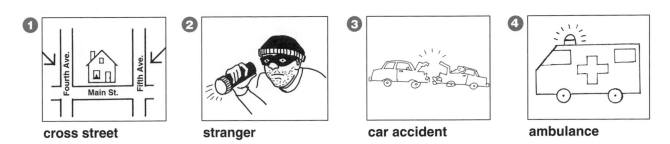

1 cross street

2 stranger

3 car accident

4 ambulance

Listen to the four conversations and number the pictures 1, 2, 3, and 4.

_____

_____

_____

_____

911 Emergency

8. Listen to Maria again and complete the conversation.

911: 911 emergency.

Maria: Hello. There's a _____ in my apartment building.

911: What's your name?

Maria: Maria Lopez.

911: What's your address?

Maria: _____ Main _____ , Apartment _____ .

911: What's the _____ _____ ?

Maria: Broadway.

911: OK. A _____ _____ is on the way.

Maria: Thank you.

9. Complete the conversation with information about yourself. Then practice it with a partner.

911: 911 emergency.

Caller: Hello. I need help. There's a _____ in my _____ .

911: What's your name?

Caller: _____ .

911: What's your address?

Caller: _____ .

911: What's the cross street?

Caller: _____ .

911: Okay. A _____ is on the way.

Caller: Thank you

 How do you report an emergency in your country?

Your Family

1. Look at the picture. Answer your teacher's questions. **(Teacher, see page 191.)**

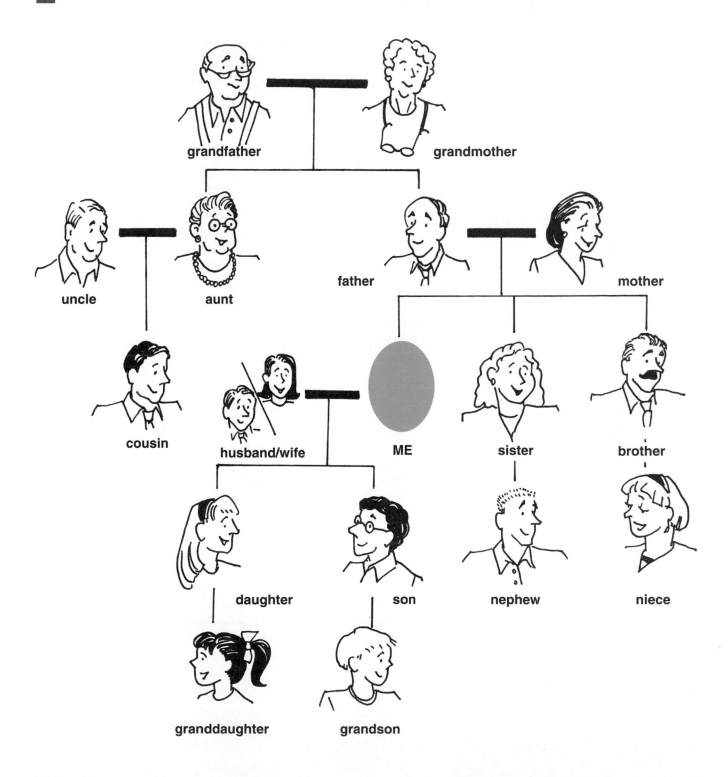

Topic: family tree
Life skill: postal services
Structure: present tense

2. Listen to John talk about his family and write the missing words.

I come from a big family. I have three _____ and four brothers. My

_____ live just a few blocks away from my house. My grandparents

also live in the neighborhood. My _____ is very old, but he goes to

work every day. And my _____ goes dancing with my _____ .

He's not married. He's single. My _____ , May, comes from China,

and she likes big families. We have three _____ , but Zabu also

thinks he's one of our _____ !

```
grandmother and grandfather = grandparents
mother and father = parents
children = kids
```

3. Complete the sentences.

1. Your father's mother is your _____ .

2. Your daughter's children are your _____ .

3. Your sister's son is your _____ .

4. Your son's sister is your _____ .

5. Your father's parents are your _____ .

6. Your cousin's sister is your _____ .

7. Your aunt's husband is your _____ .

8. Your parents' only child is _____ .

What Does Jody's Uncle Do?

4. Look at the picture. Answer your teacher's questions. **(Teacher, see page 191.)**

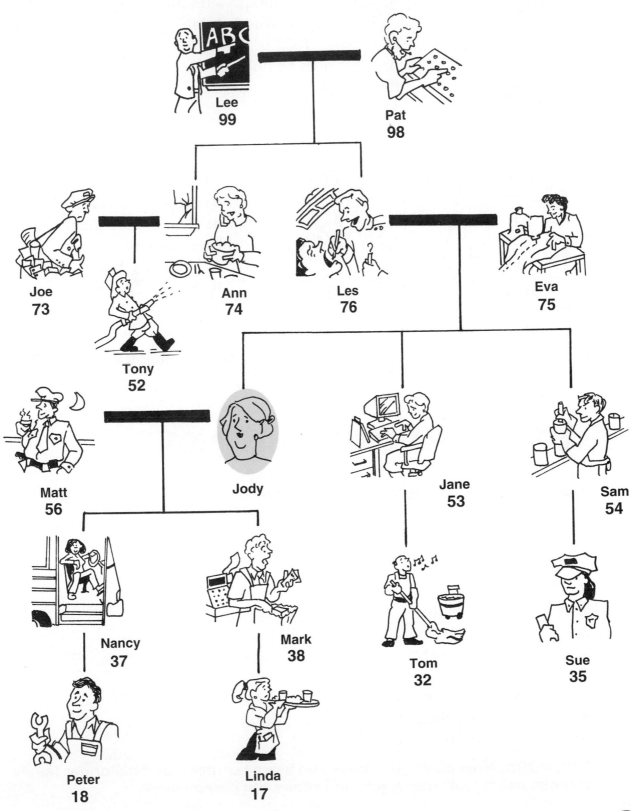

Lee
99

Pat
98

Joe
73

Tony
52

Ann
74

Les
76

Eva
75

Matt
56

Jody

Jane
53

Sam
54

Nancy
37

Mark
38

Tom
32

Sue
35

Peter
18

Linda
17

Conversation

5. Listen to the conversation. Then practice it with your teacher.

Les-76

A: Jody, tell me about your family.
  What's your father's name?
B: Les.
A: What does he do?
B: He's a dentist.
A: How old is he?
B: He's 76.

Nancy-37

Mark-38

A: What are your kids' names?
B: Nancy and Mark.
A: How old are they?
B: 37 and 38.
A: What do they do?
B: Nancy is a bus driver and Mark
  is a cashier at a store.

PAIRWORK. Now look at page 119. Make new conversations with a partner. Ask about Jody's family.

Learn about Your Classmates

6. Practice the conversation with your teacher.

A: Do you have a sister?
B: Yes, I do.
A: What's her name?
B: Helen.
A: Where does she live?
B: In New York.
A: What does she do?
B: She's a teacher.
A: What's your father's name?
B: My father isn't living.
A: Oh. I'm sorry to hear that.

PAIRWORK. Now close your book and ask a partner about his or her family. You can ask about: name, job, and where the person lives.

At the Post Office

7. Learn the new words. Look at the pictures. Repeat the words after your teacher.

  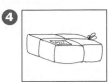

stamp   aerogram   money order   package   airmail

Listen to the four conversations and number the pictures 1, 2, 3, and 4.

_____

$ _____

_____

$ _____

_____

$ _____

_____

$ _____

Listen again. Write how much things cost.

At the Post Office

8. Stan is at the post office. He is sending money to his brother. Listen to his conversation. Then practice it with your teacher and a partner.

Clerk: Can I help you?
Stan: Yes. Can I have a money order, please?
Clerk: For how much?
Stan: $400.00.
Clerk: $400.00. Here you are. Print the names and addresses on **both** sides.
Stan: OK. Thank you.

9. Look at the money order with your partner. Ask your teacher if you have any questions.

Now fill out the money order. Print the name and address of a family member or a friend on the left side. Print your name and address on the right.

✉	**UNITED STATES POSTAL MONEY ORDER**	15-800 / 000

490 73078 248   931204   941331 8

SERIAL NUMBER	YEAR, MONTH, DAY	POST OFFICE	U.S. DOLLARS AND CENTS
PAY TO		CHECKWRITER IMPRINT AREA	$
ADDRESS		FROM	
		ADDRESS	
COD NO. OR USED FOR			

⑆00000800 2⑈   490 73078 248⑈

How do people send money in your country?

What Do They Do?
What Are They Doing?

1. Look at the pictures. Answer your teacher's questions. **(Teacher, see page 192.)**

MOST SUMMERS	THIS SUMMER

July 1 – July 21

July 1 – July 15

July 1 – Aug. 1

July 1 – July 10

Topic: vacation activities
Life skill: first aid
Structure: present tense versus
present continuous tense

123

A Special Trip

2. **Listen to your teacher. Repeat the sentences.**

❶

Most Summers

The kids ride horses at summer camp for three weeks.
They go with their classmates and eat terrible food.

❷

This Summer

The kids are camping in Alaska for two weeks with their parents.
They're eating a lot of barbecued hamburgers.

❸

Most Summers

Stan relaxes at his mother's house for a month.
He goes with his sister and eats spaghetti every day. (His mother loves spaghetti.)

❹

This Summer

Stan is playing golf in Hawaii and he's staying for ten days.
He's alone and he's eating a lot of seafood.

PAIRWORK. Now look at page 123. Make new sentences with a partner.

3. Listen to the questions and answers. Repeat them after your teacher.

MOST SUMMERS	THIS SUMMMER

MOST SUMMERS

A: What **do** they do?
B: Ride horses.

THIS SUMMMER

A: What **are** they **doing**?
B: Camping.

A: Where do they go?
B: To summer camp.

A: Where are they camping?
B: In Alaska.

July 1–August 1

A: How long does Stan stay there?
B: A month.

July 1–July 10

A: How long is Stan staying?
B: Ten days.

A: What kind of food does he eat?
B: Spaghetti.

A: What kind of food is he eating?
B: Seafood.

A: Who does he go with?
B: His sister.

A: Who is he going with?
B: Nobody. He's going alone.

Now look at page 123. Answer your teacher's questions about the pictures.

4. Practice the conversations with your teacher.

A: What are the kids doing this summer?
B: Camping.
A: Who are they camping with?
B: Their parents.

A: What does Stan do most summers?
B: He relaxes at his mother's house.
A: What kind of food does he eat?
B: Spaghetti.

PAIRWORK. Now look at page 123. Make new conversations with a partner.

Learn about Your Classmates

5. Practice the conversations with your teacher.

A: What do you usually do on the weekends?
B: Most weekends I stay home and watch TV.
A: What are you doing this weekend?
B: I'm seeing a movie.

A: What do you usually do in the evening?
B: Most evenings I watch TV with my children.
A: What are you doing this evening?
B: I'm going out with my wife.

A: What do you usually do in the summer?
B: Most summers I relax and work in the yard.
A: What are you doing this summer?
B: Same as usual.

Close your book. Make new conversations with a partner. Ask about:
1. most weekends/this weekend; 2. most evenings/this evening;
3. most summers/this summer

First Aid

6. Learn the new words. Look at the pictures. Repeat the words after your teacher. Then practice the conversation.

1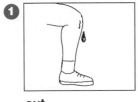
cut

2
burn

3
bee sting

4
the chills

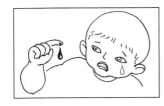

A: Why is the baby crying?
B: He has a cut on his finger.
A: A cut? **Poor** baby!

 7. John and his family are camping. Listen and draw a line from the person to the problem he or she has.

1. Tim

2. Kate

3. Ben

4. Zabu

Do people go camping in your country?

First Aid

8. Learn the new words. Look at the pictures. Repeat the words after your teacher.

1 Band-Aid

2 ice

3 cream

4 blanket

Listen to the conversations and write the missing words.

1. **A:** I have a _____ on my finger.
   B: A cut? You need a _____.
   A: Yeah. Can you please get me one?
   B: Sure.

2. **A:** I have a _____ on my face.
   B: A bee sting? You need _____.
   A: Yeah. Can you please get me some?
   B: Sure.

9. Look at the pictures and write new conversations. Then practice them with a partner.

1. **A:** ___I have_____
   B: _____
   A: _____
   B: _____

2. **A:** ___I have_____
   B: _____
   A: _____
   B: _____

UNIT 21

At the Doctor

1. Learn the new words. Listen to the words. Repeat them after your teacher.
(Teacher, see page 193.)

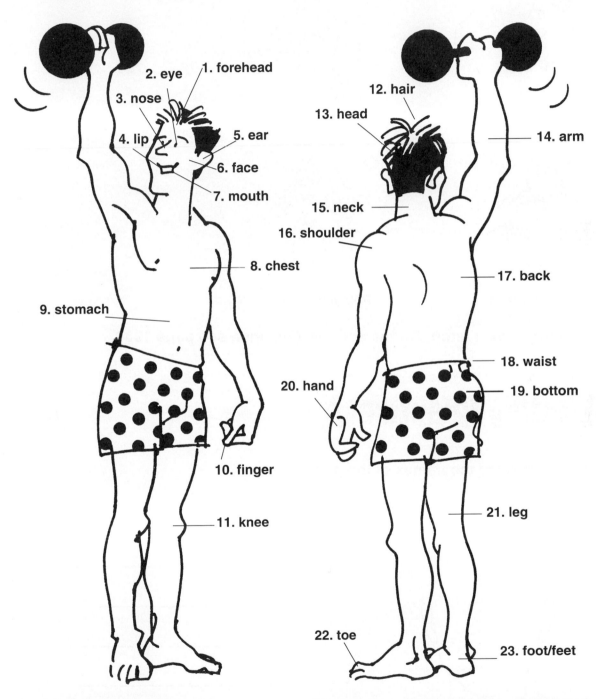

1. forehead
2. eye
3. nose
4. lip
5. ear
6. face
7. mouth
8. chest
9. stomach
10. finger
11. knee
12. hair
13. head
14. arm
15. neck
16. shoulder
17. back
18. waist
19. bottom
20. hand
21. leg
22. toe
23. foot/feet

PAIRWORK. Practice with a partner. Student A, read the words. Student B, look at the pictures and point to the correct part.

Topic: body parts
Life skill: medical checkup
Structure: imperatives

 129

Your Body

2. Listen to the sentences. Repeat them after your teacher.

1

Touch your nose.

2

Scratch your back.

3

Cover your eyes.

4

Rub your neck.

Close your book. Listen. Do the actions. **(Teacher, see page 193.)**

Writing Practice

3. Draw a face. Write the names of the parts.

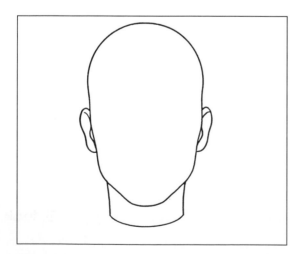

_____

_____

_____

_____

_____

_____

Making a Doctor's Appointment

4. John isn't feeling well. Listen to his conversation with the nurse and practice it with your teacher.

Nurse: Hello. Dr. Brown's office.
John: Hello. This is John Phillips. I'm not feeling well. I want an appointment with the doctor, please.
Nurse: What's wrong?
John: My back hurts.
Nurse: Can you come at 4:00 on Friday?
John: 4:00 on Friday? Sure.
Nurse: OK. Goodbye.

5. May and the children aren't feeling well. Listen to the conversations and write the information.

	What hurts	Day and time of appointment
1. May	head	Wednesday 9:00
2. Tim		
3. Kate		
4. Ben		

In your country, is it expensive to go to the doctor? Who pays the doctor?

Making a Doctor's Appointment

6. Practice making a doctor's appointment with a partner. Look at the pictures and make four conversations.

Nurse: Hello. Dr. Smith's office.

You: Hello. This is _____ _____ .
I'm not feeling well. I want an
appointment with the doctor, please.

Nurse: What's wrong?

You: My _____ hurts.

Nurse: Can you come at _____ on _____?

You: _____ on _____ ? Sure.

Nurse: OK. Goodbye.

 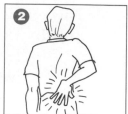

7. Fill out the form.

Patient Information

Name: _____
    (first)   (middle)   (last)

Address: _____

Phone #:_____ Soc. Sec. #: _____

Age: _____ Birthdate: _____

Sex: M F   Marital Status: married   single   No. of Children:___

Height: _____ **Weight:** _____

Are you taking any **medicine** now?   yes   no   How often? _____

	yes	no
Does your head hurt?	☐	☐
Does your back hurt?	☐	☐
Does your stomach hurt?	☐	☐
Do your ears hurt?	☐	☐
Do your eyes hurt?	☐	☐

In an emergency, call _____

---

8. Look at the pictures. Listen to the sentences. Repeat them after your teacher.

1 Open wide.

2 Say "Ahhhh!"

3 Take off your shirt.

4 Raise your arm.

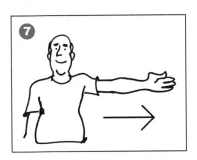

5 Lower your arm.

6 Bend your arm.

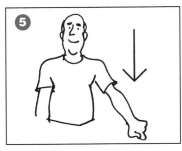

7 Straighten your arm.

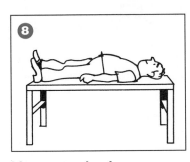

8 Lie on your back.

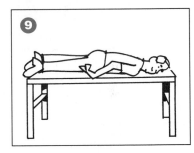

9 Lie on your stomach.

10 Breathe in.

11 Hold your breath.

12 Breathe out.

9. Close your book. Listen to your teacher. Do the actions. (Teacher, see page 193.)

Listen and Write

10. John is having a checkup. Listen to the doctor and write the number under the correct picture.

 a

 b

 c

 d

_____

_____

_____

_____

 e

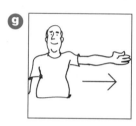 f

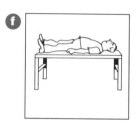 g

 h

_____

_____

_____

_____

 i

 j

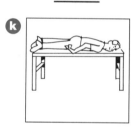 k

 l

_____

_____

_____

_____

11. Read the questions. Then write your answers.

	You	Your partner
1. How much do you weigh?	_____	_____
2. How tall are you?	_____	_____
3. Are you single or married?	_____	_____
4. How many children do you have?	_____	_____
5. How often do you have a medical checkup?	_____	_____

PAIRWORK. Now ask a partner the same questions and write his or her answers.

What's the Matter with May?

1. Look at the pictures. Answer your teacher's questions. (Teacher, see page 193.)

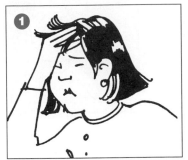

May

Pablo

Kate

Stan

Ann

Tim

Mr. Morgan

John

Tony

Jane

Maria

Mrs. Morgan

Topic: health problems
Life skill: medicines
Structure: present tense

135

Health Problems

2. Learn the new words. Listen to the sentences. Repeat them after your teacher.

1 She has a headache.
or Her head hurts.

2 He has a toothache.
or His tooth hurts.

3 She has an earache.
or Her ear hurts.

4 He has a stomachache.
or His stomach hurts.

5 She has a backache.
or Her back hurts.

6 He has a cold.
He has the flu.

7 He has a fever.
or He has a temperature.

8 He has a cough.

9 He has a sore throat.
or His throat hurts.

10 She has a rash.

11 She has diarrhea.

12 She feels dizzy.

> She has a _____ ache. = Her _____ hurts.

PAIRWORK. Practice with a partner. Student A, look at this page and say the sentences. Student B, look at page 135 and point to the pictures.

Listen and Write

3. **Listen and complete the sentences.**

1. Stan isn't feeling well. His stomach _____.

2. Tony is sick. He has a _____ _____.

3. Look at Jane's arm. She has a _____.

4. May isn't feeling well. She has a _____.

5. Tim's sleeping in bed. He has a _____.

6. Help Mrs. Morgan sit down. She feels _____.

7. Mr. Morgan is sick in bed. He has a _____.

8. John isn't feeling well. He has a _____.

Conversation

4. **Practice the conversations with your teacher.**

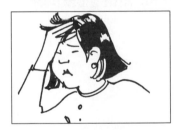

A: What's the matter with May?
B: She has a headache.
A: Oh, poor May!

A: What's the matter with Kate?
B: Her ear hurts.
A: Oh, poor Kate!

A: What's the matter with Mr. Morgan?
B: He has a fever.
A: Oh, poor Mr. Morgan!

PAIRWORK. Now look at page 135. Make new conversations with a partner.

5. Practice the conversations with your teacher.

A: I'm not feeling well.
B: What's the matter?
A: I have a toothache.
B: That's too bad! **Since when?**
A: Since Friday.

A: I'm not feeling well.
B: What's the matter?
A: My ear hurts.
B: That's too bad! Since when?
A: Since this morning.

PAIRWORK. Now look at page 135. Make new conversations with a partner.

6. PAIRWORK. Work with a partner. Read the questions and think of *possible* answers.

1. Why does May have a headache?

2. Why does Pablo's tooth hurt?

3. Why does Kate have an earache?

4. Why does Stan have a stomachache?

5. Why does Ann's back hurt?

6. Why does Tim have a cold?

7. Why does John have a cough?

8. Why does Tony have a sore throat?

With your partner, tell your classmates your answers.

Taking Your Temperature

7. Look at the thermometers. Read the sentences with your teacher.

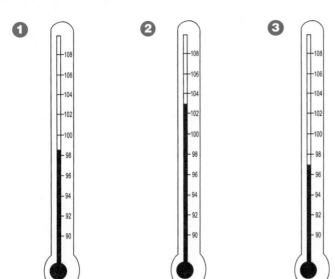

1. John's temperature is **normal**. It's 98.6° (ninety-eight point six **degrees**).

2. Mr. Morgan's temperature is **high**. It's 103°.

3. Maria's temperature is low. It's 97°.

8. Look at the thermometers. Write the temperature. Then circle *normal, high,* or *low.*

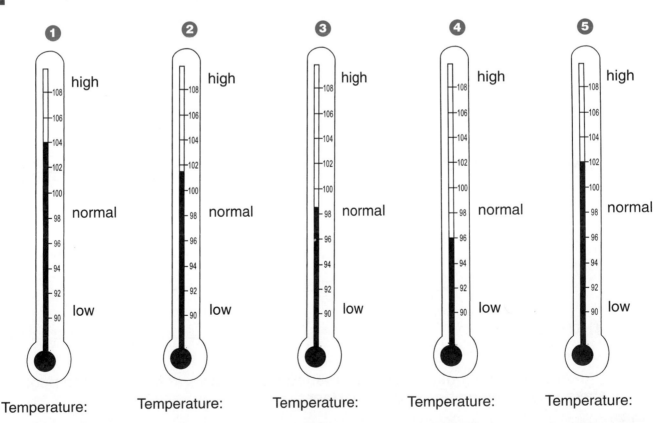

Temperature:

_____ _____ _____ _____ _____

Medicine

9. Learn the new words. Look at the pictures. Repeat the words after your teacher.

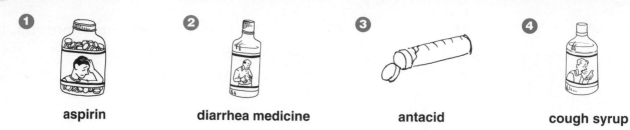

1 aspirin   **2** diarrhea medicine   **3** antacid   **4** cough syrup

May and John are talking about a health problem. Practice the conversation with your teacher.

May: I'm not feeling well.
John: What's the problem?
May: I have a headache.
John: Why don't you take some aspirin?
May: Aspirin? That's a good idea.

10. People aren't feeling well at school. Listen to the conversations and draw a line from the person to the correct health problem. Then write the medicine.

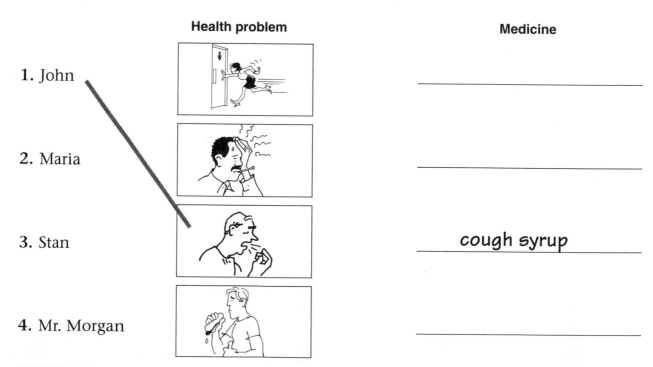

Health problem   Medicine

1. John

2. Maria

3. Stan   cough syrup

4. Mr. Morgan

PAIRWORK. Now look at the conversation and pictures at the top of the page. Make four conversations with a partner.

Is medicine in the United States different from medicine in your country?

What's Maria Going to Do Tomorrow?

1. This summer Maria is going on a **trip** to Alaska. Look at the **calendar**. Answer your teacher's questions. **(Teacher, see page 193.)**

JULY

Sunday	Monday	Tuesday	Wednesday	Thursday	Friday	Saturday
1	2	3	4	5	6	7
8	9	10 *today*	11	12	13	14
15	16	17	18	19	20	21
22	23	24	25	26	27	28
29	30	31				

Topic: future plans
Life skills: personal care; the calendar
Structure: future *going to*

141

Vacation Plans

2. Learn the new words. Listen to the words. Repeat them after your teacher.

① pack

② fly to Alaska

③ ride a horse

④ go fishing

⑤ play golf

⑥ climb a mountain

⑦ play tennis

⑧ fly back

⑨ unpack

⑩ see Stan

PAIRWORK. Practice with a partner. Student A, look at this page and say the words. Student B, look at page 141 and point to the correct picture.

Listen and Write

Use *going to* to talk about the future.

3. Listen and complete the sentences.

1. On July 19, Maria is going to _____ play tennis _____.

2. On July 12, Maria is going to _____ _____ _____.

3. On July 11, Maria is going to _____ for her trip.

4. On July 13, Maria is going to _____ _____ _____.

5. On July 14, Maria is going to _____ _____.

6. On July 17 and 18, Maria is going to _____ _____ _____.

The Calendar

4. Listen to your teacher. Repeat the words and sentences.

JULY

Sunday	Monday	Tuesday	Wednesday	Thursday	Friday	Saturday
1	2	3	4	5	6	7
8	9	10 *today*	11	12	13	14
15	16	17	18	19	20	21
22	23	24	25	26	27	28
29	30	31				

TODAY
this morning
this afternoon
tonight

1. Today is July 10.
2. What day of the week is today?
   It's Tuesday.
3. What's the date?
   It's the 10th.
4. July 11: tomorrow
5. July 12: the day after tomorrow
6. July 13:
   three days **from now** or **in** three days
7. July 17:
   one week from now or in one week
8. July 8–July 14:
   this week
9. July 15–July 21:
   next week
10. July 22–July 28:
    two weeks from now or in two weeks
11. July 14: on Saturday or this Saturday
12. July 16: next Monday
13. July 23: two weeks from now on Monday

Listen and Write

5. Listen and find the date on the calendar. Write the date.

1. _____ July 11 _____

2. _____

3. _____

4. _____

5. _____

6. _____

7. _____

8. _____

9. _____

10. _____

Conversation

Two Ways to Talk about the Future
1. **ing:** What's she do**ing** tomorrow?
2. **going to:** What's she **going to** do tomorrow?

What's she going to do _____ ?

6. Practice the conversations with your teacher.

A: What's Maria going to do this Friday?
B: Ride a horse.

A: What's she going to do next Thursday?
B: Play tennis.

PAIRWORK. Now look at page 141. Make new conversations with a partner.

Learn about Your Classmates

What are you going to do_____?

7. Practice the conversation with your teacher.

A: What are you going to do this weekend?
B: See a movie with my family.
A: What are you going to do next summer?
B: I'm not sure. Maybe go to Mexico.

Now ask three classmates about their plans for next weekend and next summer.

 Where do people go on vacation in your country?

Personal Care

8. **Learn the new words. Look at the pictures. Repeat the words after your teacher.**

    brush my teeth   shave   comb my hair   wash my hair   dry my hair

Stan is going to see Maria tomorrow. Listen to him and number the pictures 1– 5.

_____   _____

_____   _____

_____

Personal Care

9. Learn the new words. Look at the pictures. Repeat the words after your teacher.

❶ toothbrush   ❷ razor   ❸ comb   ❹ shampoo   ❺ hair dryer

10. Look at the pictures. Write what you're going to do tomorrow morning in the correct order. Then write what you're going to use.

1. _____   _____

2. _____   _____

3. _____   _____

4. _____   _____

5. _____   _____

11. Practice the conversations with your teacher.

A: What are you going to do first?
B: Wash my hair.
A: With shampoo?
B: Yes, with shampoo.

A: What are you going to do second?
B: Dry my hair.
A: With a hair dryer?
B: No, with a **towel!**

PAIRWORK. Ask a partner what he or she is going to do tomorrow morning. Use *first*, *second*, *third*, *fourth*, and *fifth*. Then answer your partner's questions.

UNIT 24

What's Going to Happen Next Monday?

1. John and Maria are talking to a **fortune-teller**. Look at the pictures. Answer your teacher's questions. (Teacher, see page 194.)

	Monday	Tuesday	Wednesday

Topic: predictions
Life skill: requesting time off work
Structure: future *going to*

147

2. Learn the new words. Listen to the words. Repeat them after your teacher.

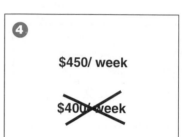

1 get a ring

2 get married

3 go to work

4 get a raise

$450/ week

$400/ week

5 buy a car

6 take the bus

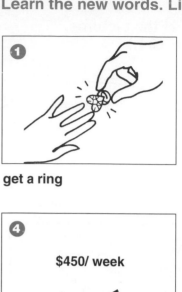

7 make a mess

8 clean (their) room

9 get in trouble

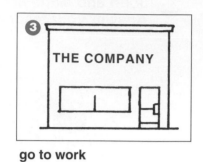

10 eat all day

11 sleep all day

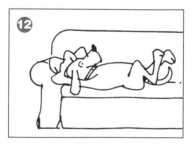

12 He isn't going to do anything.

PAIRWORK. Practice with a partner. Student A, look at this page and say the words. Student B, look at page 147 and point to the pictures.

Listen and Write

He She	is isn't	going to _____ .
They	are aren't	

3. Listen and complete the sentences.

1. On Tuesday, Maria is going to _____ *get married* _____ .

2. On Wednesday, the kids are going to _____ _____ _____ .

3. On Monday, Zabu is going to _____ _____ _____ .

4. On Wednesday, John isn't going to _____ _____ _____ .

5. On Tuesday, the kids aren't going to _____ _____ _____ .

6. On Wednesday, Maria isn't going to _____ _____ _____ .

7. On Tuesday, Zabu isn't going to _____ _____ _____ .

8. On Monday, John is going to _____ _____ _____ .

Conversation

4. Practice the conversations with your teacher.

A: What's going to happen to Maria on Monday?
B: She's going to get a ring.

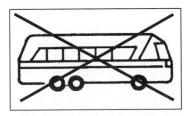

A: What's going to happen to John on Wednesday?
B: He isn't going to take the bus.

PAIRWORK. Now look at page 147. Make new conversations with a partner.

5. Look at page 147. Write sentences about next week.

Example: _____ Maria is going to get married. _____

1. _____

2. _____

3. _____

4. _____

5. _____

Learn about Your Classmates

I'm	going to not going to	_____ .

6. PAIRWORK. Tell a partner three things you are going to do next week.
Then tell three things you are *not* going to do.

Now write about next week.

Example: _____ I'm going to visit my brother. _____

1. _____

2. _____

3. _____

4. _____

5. _____

6. _____

Asking for Time Off

7. Listen to May and Maria talk to their bosses. Then practice the conversations with your teacher.

1. **May:** Can I leave work at 3:00 tomorrow?
   Boss: Why?
   May: My husband has a doctor's appointment.
   My children are going to be home alone.
   Boss: OK.
   May: Thank you.

2. **Maria:** Can I have the **day off** on Tuesday?
   Mr. Morgan: Why?
   Maria: My mother is going to be in town.
   Mr. Morgan: I'm sorry, but you can't have Tuesday off.
   We're going to be too **busy.**
   Maria: Oh well.

8. Listen to the conversations. Check *leave early* or *day off* and the correct day.

	Sun.	Mon.	Tues.	Wed.	Thurs.	Fri.	Sat.
_____ 1. leave early ✔ / day off ☐							✔
_____ 2. leave early ☐ / day off ☐							
_____ 3. leave early ☐ / day off ☐							
_____ 4. leave early ☐ / day off ☐							
_____ 5. leave early ☐ / day off ☐							

Do the people get time off? Listen again and write *yes* or *no* beside each number.

Asking for Time Off

9. Look at the pictures and complete the conversations.
Then practice them with a partner.

1. **A:** Can I _____ _____ at _____ today?

    B: Why?

    A: _____

    B: OK.

    A: Thank you.

2. **A:** Can I _____ . _____ _____ _____ on Tuesday?

    B: Why?

    A: _____ .

    B: I'm sorry, but you can't have Tuesday off.
    We're going to be too busy.

    A: Oh well.

10. Ask your boss for time off work. Write a new conversation.

You: Can I _____

Boss: Why?

You: _____

_____

_____

Boss: _____

_____

_____

You: _____

PAIRWORK. Practice your conversation with your partner.

Why do people take time off work in your country?

Can You Help Me, Please?

1. Look at the pictures. Answer your teacher's questions. **(Teacher, see page 194.)**

Topic: problems at work
Life skill: work schedule changes
requesting assistance
Structure: modal *can*

153

2. **Learn the new words. Listen to the sentences. Repeat them after your teacher.**

I can't open this bottle. It's too tight.   I can open it for you.

I can't understand these directions.   I can explain them to you.

I can't reach that box.   I can get it for you.

I can't move this box. It's too heavy.   I can help you move it.

I can't start this machine.   I can help you start it.

I can't find the sugar.   I can help you find it.

PAIRWORK. Practice with a partner. Student A, look at this page and say the sentences. Student B, look at page 153 and point to the pictures.

Listen and Write

3. Listen and complete the sentences.

1. I can't _____ these directions.

2. I can _____ them for you.

3. I can't move this desk. It's _____ _____.

4. I can _____ _____ move it.

5. I _____ open this window.

6. _____ _____ it for you.

Conversation

| Can you help me, please? | I can _____ for you.
I can help you_____ . |

4. Practice the conversations with your teacher.

Worker:	Can you help me, please?
Supervisor:	Sure. What is it?
Worker:	I can't understand these directions.
Supervisor:	I can explain them to you.
Worker:	Thanks a lot.
Supervisor:	You're welcome.

Worker:	Can you help me, please?
Coworker:	Sure. What is it?
Worker:	I can't move this box.
Coworker:	I can help you move it.
Worker:	Thanks a lot.
Coworker:	You're welcome.

PAIRWORK. Now look at page 153. Make conversations with a partner.

Can You Fix a Leaking Faucet?

5. Look at the pictures. Answer your teacher's questions. **(Teacher, see page 195.)**

①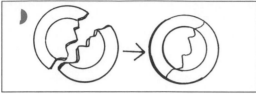

②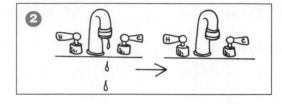

③

④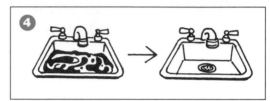

⑤

⑥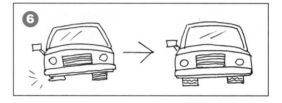

Now look at the bottom of this page. Repeat the words in the box after your teacher.

Learn about Your Classmates

Can you _____ ?	Yes, I can. No, I can't.

6. Practice the questions and answers with your teacher.

A: Can you fix a leaking faucet?
B: Yes, I can. What about you?
A: I can't.

PAIRWORK. Now look at the pictures at the top of the page and make new conversations with a partner. You can also make different *Can you . . . ?* questions with your partner. Then tell your other classmates some things your partner can and can't do.

1. fix a broken dish	2. fix a leaking faucet
3. fix a broken window	4. fix a stopped-up sink
5. Change a light bulb	6. change a tire

Schedule Changes at Work

 7. Maria and May are talking to their bosses at work. Listen to their conversations. Then practice them with your teacher.

1. **Mr. Morgan:** Can you work **overtime** tomorrow?
   Maria: Sure. No problem.

2. **Boss:**   Can you work the night shift next week?
   May: I'm sorry, but I can't. I'm staying home with my children
                   next week.
   Boss: All right.

 8. Look at the schedule changes with your teacher. Then listen to the conversations. Draw a line from the person to the schedule change. Then check *yes* or *no*.

	Schedule change	yes	no
1. Pablo	come early	☐	☐
2. Nancy	weekend	☐	☐
3. Ann	day shift	☑	☐
4. Peter	night shift	☐	☐
5. Matt	overtime	☐	☐

 Do people work overtime in your country?

Schedule Changes at Work

9. Listen to the conversations and write the missing words.

1. **A:** Can you work the _____ _____ next Saturday?

    B: Sure. No problem.

2. **A:** Can you _____ in _____ tomorrow?

    B: I'm sorry, but I can't. I'm _____ to the dentist at 11:00.

    A: All right.

3. **A:** Can you work _____ tonight?

    B: I'm sorry, _____ _____ _____ .

    I'm meeting my sister at the airport tonight.

    A: All right.

10. Make conversations with a partner about schedule changes at work.

1. **A:** Can you _____

    B: Sure. No problem.

2. **A:** Can you _____

    B: I'm sorry, but I can't.

    I'm _____

    A: All right.

Now complete the conversations above.

UNIT 26

Where Did Maria Go Yesterday?

1. Look at the calendar. Answer your teacher's questions. **(Teacher, see page 195.)**

AUGUST

Sunday	Monday	Tuesday	Wednesday	Thursday	Friday	Saturday
		1	2	3	4	5
6	7	8	9	10	11	12
13	14	15	16	17	18	19
20	21	22	23	24	25	26
27	28	29	30	31		

Topic: past events
Life skills: eating out; the calendar
Structure: past tense

159

The Calendar

2. Listen to your teacher. Repeat the words and sentences.

			AUGUST			
Sunday	Monday	Tuesday	Wednesday	Thursday	Friday	Saturday
		1	2	3	4	5
6	7	8	9	10	11	12
13	14	15	16	17	18	19
20	21	22	23	24 *today*	25	26
27	28	29	30	31		

1. August 23: yesterday
2. August 22: the day before yesterday
3. August 21: three days **ago**
4. August 17: one week ago
5. August 20–August 26: this week
6. August 13–August 19: last week
7. August 6–August 12: two weeks ago
8. August 21: on Monday
9. August 14: last Monday
10. August 7: two weeks ago on Monday

> **YESTERDAY**
> **yesterday morning**
> **yesterday afternoon**
> **last night**

Listen and Write

3. Listen and find the date on the calendar. Write the date below.

1. _____August 15_____

2. _____

3. _____

4. _____

5. _____

6. _____

7. _____

8. _____

9. _____

10. _____

Two Weeks' Activities

4. Do you remember these places? Listen to your teacher and point to the correct picture.

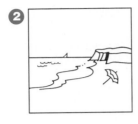
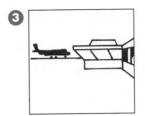

Listen and Write

5. Listen and fill in the blanks.

1. Where did Maria go _____*yesterday*_____? To a restaurant.

2. Where did Maria go _____ _____ _____? To the hospital.

3. Where did Maria go _____ _____ _____? To the zoo.

4. Where did Maria go _____ _____? To a party.

5. Where did Maria go _____ _____? To the hair salon.

6. Where did Maria go _____ _____ _____ _____?
   To the bank.

7. Where did Maria go _____ _____? To the park.

> **Use *did* to ask about the past.**

Conversation

Where **did** she go . . . ?

6. Practice the conversations with your teacher.

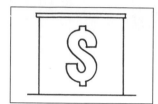

A: Where did Maria go the day before yesterday?
B: To the bank.

A: Where did Maria go last Wednesday?
B: Nowhere.

PAIRWORK. Now look at page 159. Make new conversations with a partner.

Learn about Your Classmates

Where **did** you go . . .?

7. Practice the conversations with your teacher.

A: Where did you go last Sunday?   **A:** Where did you go last summer?
B: To the park.   **B:** Nowhere.

Now ask three classmates *Where did you go?* and write their answers below.

	Classmate 1	Classmate 2	Classmate 3
last Sunday			
last summer			
two weeks ago			
the day before yesterday			
on Saturday			

At a Restaurant

8. Look at the menu. Repeat the names of the foods after your teacher.

Mr. D's Restaurant
MENU

MAIN DISHES		SANDWICHES	
Fried chicken	$5.95	Hamburger	$2.25
Roast beef	$7.25	Cheeseburger	$2.95
Fish	$6.50	Hot dog	$1.95
Spaghetti	$4.75		

SIDE DISHES		DRINKS	
Tossed salad	$1.75	Soda	$ .70
Vegetable soup	$2.00	Coffee	$ .60
Baked Potato	$1.50	Tea	$ .60
French fries	$ .95	Juice	$1.00

9. Maria is at Mr. D's Restaurant. Listen to her conversation with the waitress. Then practice it with your teacher.

Waitress: Hello. Are you ready to **order**?

Maria: Yes. I'd like the fried chicken.

Waitress: Anything else?

Maria: French fries.

Waitress: Anything to drink?

Maria: Coffee, please.

Waitress: Thank you.

PAIRWORK. With a partner, order dinner from the menu. Student A is the waitress. Student B is the **customer.** Then change. Student B is the waitress. Student A is the customer.

Now, listen to Maria talk to the waitress after dinner. Then practice the conversation with your teacher.

Maria: Can I have the check, please?

Waitress: Sure. Thank you.

At a Restaurant

10. Stan is asking Maria about her dinner last night. Listen to the conversation and practice it with your teacher.

Stan: What restaurant did you go to?

Maria: Mr. D's.

Stan: How did you get there?

Maria: By bus.

Stan: What did you order?

Maria: Fried chicken, french fries, and coffee.

Stan: How much did it cost?

Maria: $8.00.

11. Read the questions with your teacher. Then ask a partner and write his or her answers. Write short answers.

1. What restaurant did you go to last? _____

2. When did you go? _____

3. How did you get there? _____

4. Who did you go with? _____

5. What did you order? _____

6. How much did it cost? _____

 Do people go out to eat often in your country? What kind of food is popular?

What Did John Do Last Week?

1. Look at the pictures. Answer your teacher's questions. **(Teacher, see page 195.)**

Topic: past events
Life skills: calling in sick
Structure: past tense

A Hard Week

2. Learn the new words. Listen to the words. Repeat them after your teacher.

  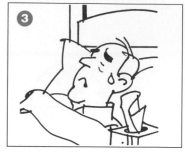

cough all day

call in sick

rest in bed

argue

cry

stay home

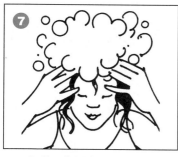  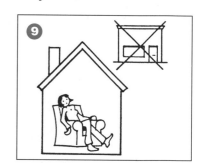

wash (her) hair

dance all night

miss work

  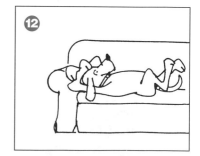

play with the kids

bark at the mail carrier

He didn't do anything.

PAIRWORK. Practice with a partner. Student A, look at this page and say the words. Student B, look at page 165 and point to the pictures.

Spelling

Use **-ed** to talk about the past.

A. brush → brush**ed**
   dance → danc**ed**

B. cry → cr**ied**
   └ consonant + y
   play play**ed**
   └ vowel + y

C. rub → ru**bb**ed
   └ 1 consonant
   └ 1 vowel
   stop → sto**pp**ed
   └ 1 consonant
   └ 1 vowel

3. Add **-ed** to these words. Follow the examples above.

1. ask _____

2. study_____

3. cook _____

4. stop _____

5. clean _____

6. play_____

7. argue _____

8. hug _____

9. call _____

10. stay_____

11. dry _____

12. wash _____

Listen and Write

4. Listen and complete the sentences.

1. Last Thursday, May____*danced*____all night.

2. Last Tuesday, John _____all day.

3. Last Tuesday, Zabu _____with the kids.

4. Maria and Stan _____ last Tuesday.

5. Last Wednesday, Maria and Stan_____ because they argued.

6. John _____ _____ _____ last Wednesday.

7. John _____ _____last Thursday.

8. Last Thursday, Zabu _____ _____ _____ all day long.

Conversation

What **did**	he she they	do. . . ?

5. Practice the conversations with your teacher.

A: What did John do last Thursday?
B: He rested in bed.

A: What did Maria and Stan do last Tuesday?
B: They argued.

A: What did May do last Wednesday?
B: She danced all night.

PAIRWORK. Now look at page 165. Make new conversations with a partner.

Calling in Sick

6. John is calling in sick. Listen to the conversation and practice it with your teacher.

Maria: English Language School. Maria speaking.
John: Hello, Maria. This is John Phillips. I can't come to work today. I'm sick.
Maria: That's too bad. What's the problem?
John: I have a fever.
Maria: Oh. Are you coming back tomorrow?
John: I hope so.
Maria: OK. I hope you **feel better.**
John: Thanks. Goodbye.

Calling in Sick

7. Listen to other people call in sick. Put a check (✔) above their problem.
Then circle *yes, no,* or *maybe.*

Coming back tomorrow?

1. Mark   yes   no   (maybe)

2. Peter   yes   no   maybe

3. Sam   yes   no   maybe

4. Eva   yes   no   maybe

5. Stan   yes   no   maybe

8. You are calling in sick. Complete the conversation and practice it with a partner.

Boss: _____ _____ speaking.

You: Hello, _____ . This is _____ .

I can't _____ . I'm sick.

Boss: That's too bad. What's the problem?

You: I have _____ .

Boss: Oh. Are you coming back tomorrow?

You: _____ .

Boss: OK. I hope you feel better.

You: _____ . _____ .

In your country, do people have to wait a long time to see the doctor?

Irregular Words in the Past	
go → went see → saw am, is → was	eat → ate have → had are → were

9. Read what happened to John last week.

Last week, John was sick. On Tuesday, he had a cough, but he went to work. On Wednesday, he also had a fever, so he called in sick. He talked to Maria at the office. Then he called his doctor to make an appointment for the afternoon. At 2:30, he went downtown to the doctor's office. Lots of people were there, so John waited a long time. At 3:30, he saw the doctor. After his appointment, he went back home. Then he ate some chicken soup. May says that chicken soup is very good medicine! On Thursday and Friday, John rested in bed and watched TV. By Saturday, he was better.

10. Look at the pictures below. Write about what you did the last time you missed work.

   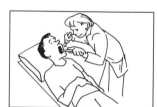

_____

_____

_____

_____

Tapescript

3. Listen and number the pictures.

1. A: Where are you from?
   B: Pardon me?
   A: Where are you from?

2. A: How old are you?
   B: Excuse me?
   A: How old are you?

3. A: What do you do?
   B: Pardon me?
   A: What's your job?

4. A: Where do you live?
   B: Pardon me?
   A: What's your address?

5. A: What's your telephone number?
   B: My what?
   A: Your phone number.

6. A: Could you tell me your area code, please?
   B: Pardon me?
   A: Your area code.

7. A: When were you born?
   B: Excuse me?
   A: Your birthday.

8. A: What's your zip code?
   B: My what?
   A: What's your zip code?

9. A: Are you married?
   B: Pardon me?
   A: Are you married or single?

10. A: What's your social security number?
    B: My what?
    A: Your social security number.

UNIT 2, P. 18

3. Listen and complete the sentences.

1. Pablo is at ___school___ .

2. Mr. and Mrs. Morgan are at ___the airport___ .

3. Ann is at ___the park___ .

4. Tony and Mark are at ___the movie theater___ .

5. Nancy and Matt are at ___a party___ .

6. Jane is at ___the bus stop___ .

7. May and Baby Ben are at ___home___ .

8. Maria is at ___the hospital___ .

UNIT 2, P. 21

7. Learn the new words. Look at the pictures. Repeat the words after your teacher. Then listen to John's conversation with the clerk. Draw a line from the food to the correct aisle.

John: Excuse me, Miss. Can you help me?
Clerk: Sure.
John: I need milk. Where's the milk?
Clerk: The milk's on aisle 6.
John: Aisle 6. Thanks. Excuse me, Miss. Can you help me?
Clerk: Sure.
John: Where are the tomatoes?
Clerk: The tomatoes? They're on aisle 1.
John: Aisle 1. Thanks. Excuse me, Miss. Can you help me?
Clerk: Sure.
John: Where's the oil?
Clerk: The oil is on aisle 5.
John: Five. OK. Ummm. Excuse me, Miss. Can you help me?
Clerk: Of course.
John: Where's the jam?
Clerk: Aisle 3. The jam's on aisle 3.
John: Three. Great. Excuse me, Miss. Can you . . .
Clerk: Yes?
John: Where are the beans?
Clerk: The beans are on aisle 2. Anything else?
John: Aisle 2. OK. I think that's it. No, wait. I need cereal too.
Clerk: The cereal is on aisle 4.
John: Four. Wonderful. That's it. Oh no! Where's my money?
Clerk: Oh no!

UNIT 3, P. 26

7. John is talking with a salesclerk. Read the questions. Then listen to each conversation. After you listen, write the answers.

1. Clerk: Can I help you?
   John: Yes. I want a blouse for my daughter, but this one is too small.
   Clerk: What size is it?
   John: Size 6. My daughter wears size 8.
   Clerk: I'm sorry. We don't have size 8.

2. Clerk: Can I help you?
   John: Yes. I want a skirt for my daughter, but this one is too big.
   Clerk: What size is it?
   John: Size 12. My daughter wears size 8.
   Clerk: I'm sorry. We don't have size 8.

3. Clerk: Can I help you?
   John: Yes. I like this dress. How much is it?
   Clerk: $30.00.
   John: $30.00? That's too expensive.

4. Clerk: Can I help you?
   John: Yes. How much is this blue jacket?
   Clerk: $25.00.
   John: OK. I'll take it.
   Clerk: Is that a dog?

John: A dog?
Clerk: That dog is in this store!
John: In this store? Oh no! Zabu!
What are *you* doing here?
Clerk: Is that your dog?
John: Yes, it is. I'm sorry. Zabu, come on.
Let's go home. I'm really *very* sorry .

UNIT 4, P. 30

3. Now listen and write the letters

1. Write the letter *A* inside the circle.
2. Write the letter *B* above the square.
3. Write the letter *C* under the triangle.
4. Write the letter *D* between the circle and the square.
5. Write the letter *E* next to the circle.
6. Write the letter *F* in the corner of the square.
7. Write the letter *G* beside the square.
8. Write the letter *H* inside the triangle.
9. Write the letter *J* below the circle.
10. Write the letter *K* outside the square, at the corner of the square.
11. Write the letter *L* over the circle.
12. Write a big letter *O* around the triangle.

UNIT 4, P. 32

7. Listen to the conversations. Draw a line from the picture to the correct location.

1. **A:** Excuse me. Where are the men's shoes?
   B: Men's shoes are on the third floor beside the coats.
   A: Beside the coats?
   B: Yes.
   A: Thank you.
   B: You're welcome.

2. **A:** Excuse me. Is the men's room on the third floor?
   B: No, it isn't. The men's room is on the first floor.
   A: Near the elevator?
   B: Yes. It's in the corner next to the elevator.
   A: Thank you.
   B: You're welcome.

3. **A:** Excuse me. Where are the skirts?
   B: Skirts are on the second floor between dresses and pants.
   A: Between dresses and pants?
   B: Yes. In front of the escalator.
   A: Thank you.
   B: You're welcome.

4. **A:** Is the women's underwear on the second floor?
   B: No, it isn't. The women's underwear is on the first floor.
   A: Behind the escalator?
   B: No. It's in front of the escalator next to the socks.

A: In front of the escalator next to the socks. O.K. Thank you.
B: You're welcome.

5. **A:** Excuse me. Where's the men's underwear?
   B: It's on the third floor, I think.
   A: On the third floor. Thanks!
   A: Excuse me! The men's underwear is *not* on the third floor.
   B: Not on the third floor? Hmmm. Then it's on the *first* floor.
   A: Next to socks?
   B: Yeah. Next to socks.
   A: Excuse me! The men's underwear is *not* next to socks!
   B: It isn't?
   A: Where is your boss?
   B: My boss? I don't work here, sir.
   A: You don't work here?
   C: Excuse me, sir. The men's underwear is on the first floor in front of the elevator. It's behind you.
   A: Behind me? Oh yeah. Here it is . . .

UNIT 5, P. 36

3. Listen and complete the sentences.

1. John is __teach__ ing a lesson to his class.

2. Mr. and Mrs. Morgan are __meet__ ing a friend at the airport.

3. Baby Ben is __sleep__ ing at home.

4. Jane is __wait__ ing for the bus.

5. Maria is __visit__ ing a friend at the hospital.

6. Tom and Sue are __buy__ ing food at the store.

7. Tony and Mark are __watch__ ing a movie at the theater.

UNIT 6, P. 42

3. Listen and complete the questions.

1. Who's __taking__ a shower?   Lee is.

2. Who's __cooking__ a meal?   Stan is.

3. Who's __getting__ dressed?   Pablo is.

4. Who's __writing__ a letter?   Ann is.

5. Who's __drinking__ coffee?   Peter is.

6. Who's __cleaning__ the house?   John is.

UNIT 7, P. 47

5. John is talking with Maria about his family. Listen to the conversations and draw a line from the person to the correct feeling.

1. **Maria:** How's your wife?
   John: Not so good.
   Maria: Oh? What's wrong?
   John: She's worried about work.
   Maria: Worried? That's too bad.

2. **Maria:** How's your son?
   John: Not so good.
   Maria: Oh? What's wrong?
   John: He's confused at school.
   Maria: Confused? That's too bad.

3. **Maria:** How's your mother?
   John: She's sleeping.
   Maria: What? At 1:00 in the afternoon?
   John: Yes. She's very tired.

4. **Maria:** How's your brother?
   John: Not so good.
   Maria: Oh? What's wrong?
   John: He's angry with his daughter.
   Maria: Angry? That's too bad.

5. **Maria:** How's Zabu?
   John: He's fine.
   Maria: That's good. What's he doing?
   John: Eating, of course!

UNIT 7, P. 48

6. Listen to the conversations and write the missing words. Then practice the conversations with a partner.

1. **Maria:** How's your daughter?
   John: She's <u>fine</u>.
   Maria: That's <u>good</u>.

2. **Maria:** <u>How's your</u> wife?
   John: Not so good.
   Maria: Oh? <u>What's wrong?</u>
   John: She's worried about work.
   Maria: Worried? That's <u>too bad.</u>

UNIT 8, P. 54

7. Listen to the four conversations. Number the places Maria is going.

1. **A:** Hello?
   B: Hello. Is Maria there?
   A: This is Maria speaking.
   B: Oh hi, Maria. This is Nancy.
   A: Hi, Nancy. Listen. I'm on my way out the door.
   B: You are? Where are you going?
   A: To the airport.
   B: To the airport?
   A: Yes. I'm going to Canada this week.
   B: Oh. Well, have fun.

   A: Thanks. Talk to you later!
   B: OK. Goodbye.

2. **A:** Hello?
   B: Hello. Is Maria there?
   A: This is Maria speaking.
   B: Oh hello, Maria. This is Mrs. Morgan.
   A: Hi, Mrs. Morgan. Listen. I'm on my way out the door.
   B: You are? Where are you going?
   A: To school.
   B: To school.
   A: Yes. I'm taking a dance class this semester.
   B: Oh. Well, have fun.
   A: Thanks. Talk to you later!
   B: OK. Goodbye.

3. **A:** Hello?
   B: Hello. Is Maria there?
   A: This is Maria speaking.
   B: Oh hi, Maria. This is Peter.
   A: Hi, Peter. Listen. I'm on my way out the door.
   B: You are? Where are you going?
   A: To the park.
   B: To the park?
   A: Yes. For a baseball game.
   B: Oh. Well, have fun!
   A: Thanks. Talk to you later!
   B: OK. Goodbye.

4. **A:** Hello?
   B: Hello. Is Maria there?
   A: This is Maria speaking.
   B: Oh hi, Maria. This is Stan.
   A: Hi Stan. Listen. I'm on my way out the door.
   B: You are? Where are you going?
   A: To a movie.
   B: To a movie? Who are you going with?
   A: With a friend.
   C: Hey, Maria. Are you home? It's Pablo!
   B: Pablo? Who's there? Who's Pablo?
   A: Listen, Stan. Talk to you later, OK?

Listen again and number the people.

UNIT 9, P. 60

10. Look at the pictures. Listen to the conversations and check the correct boxes.

1. **A:** Excuse me. Is there a pay phone around here?
   B: Yes, there is. Go 3 blocks and turn left.
   A: Three blocks and turn left. Thank you.

2. **A:** Excuse me. Is there a health clinic around here?
   B: Yes, there is. Go 5 blocks and turn right.
   A: Five blocks and turn right. Thank you.

3. **A:** Excuse me. Is there a library around here?
   B: Yes, there is. Go 2 blocks and turn right.
   A: Two blocks and turn right. Thank you.

4. **A:** Excuse me. Is there a Chinese restaurant around here?

B: Yes, there is. Go 4 blocks and turn left.
A: Four blocks and turn left. Thank you.

5. A: Excuse me. Is there a beach around here?
   B: A beach? In the city? No, there isn't.
   A: Hmmm. Is there a zoo around here?
   B: A zoo? With animals, you mean?
   A: Yeah, a zoo.
   B: No, there isn't.
   A: Too bad. I'm looking for someplace fun.
   B: Well, there *is* a movie theater.
   A: A movie theater? Where is it?
   B: Go 2 blocks and turn left.
   A: Two blocks and turn left. Thank you!
   A: Oh no! The movie's in Chinese! I don't speak Chinese!

UNIT 10, P. 65

3. Listen to John and May. Draw a line from the picture to the correct location.

1. **John:** Honey, where's my watch?
   May: In the kitchen.
   John: Well, I'm in the kitchen, but I don't see my watch.
   May: Is it on the refrigerator?
   John: No.
   May: How about the counter? Is it on the counter next to the sink?
   John: No, it isn't next to the sink. Oh, here it is. It's on the microwave.

2. **John:** I can't find my shoes.
   May: Which shoes?
   John: My brown shoes.
   May: Look in the bathroom.
   John: The bathroom?
   John: I don't see them anywhere.
   May: Are they beside the bathtub?
   John: No.
   May: Are they under the sink?
   John: No. Hey, wait a minute. Here they are behind the toilet. Now what are they doing behind the toilet?

3. **John:** Where's my hat?
   May: I don't know. Look in the living room.
   John: Well, I'm in the living room. Now what?
   May: Is it in the closet?
   John: No, it isn't in the closet.
   May: Is it on the sofa?
   John: No. And it isn't on the floor . . . Oh. There it is. It's on the stairs.

4. **John:** Honey, where are my blue socks?
   May: You know where they are!
   John: I'm *in* the bedroom, and I'm *looking* in my dresser. But my blue socks aren't here.
   May: Well, then, maybe they're inside *my* dresser.
   John: They aren't in your dresser.
   John: Sorry, Zabu. Oh, no!
   May: What's wrong?
   John: My blue socks! Zabu's sleeping on them! They're under Zabu!

UNIT 10, P. 66

6. Listen to the telephone conversation and write the missing words. Then practice it with your partner.

Manager: Hello.
Nancy: Hello. Is the manager there?
Manager: Speaking.
Nancy: I'm <u>looking</u> for an apartment.
Manager: How many bedrooms?
Nancy: <u>One.</u>
Manager: There's a <u>one</u>-bedroom apartment on Polk Street.
Nancy: Is there a <u>washer and dryer?</u>
Manager: Yes, there is.
Nancy: Are there many <u>cupboards</u> in the kitchen?
Manager: No, there aren't. Any other questions?
Nancy: No. But <u>thank you</u> for the information.
Manager: You're welcome. Goodbye.

UNIT 11, P. 70

2. Listen and number the pictures.

1. A: What time are Tony and Mark going to the movies tonight?
   B: At seven thirty.

2. A: What time is Maria visiting her friend in the hospital tomorrow?
   B: I think she's going at eleven fifteen.

3. A: What time are Nancy and Matt going to the party tonight?
   B: They're going at eight forty-five.

4. A: What time is Stan going to the laundromat tomorrow?
   B: I think he's going at a quarter after ten.

5. A: What time are Mr. and Mrs. Morgan going fishing on Saturday?
   B: They're going at half past one.

6. A: What time is Maria playing baseball tomorrow?
   B: At noon.

Listen again and number the clocks.

UNIT 11, P. 70

3. Listen. Draw the hands on the clocks.

1. A: What time is it, please?
   B: It's nine forty-five.

2. A: Do you have the time, please?
   B: Yes. It's eight thirty.

3. A: Excuse me. Do you know the time?
   B: Let's see . . . It's four fifteen.

4. A: What time is it, please?
   B: It's a quarter after three.

5. A: Do you have the time, please?
   B: Um hum. Oh my! It's midnight!

6. A: Excuse me. Do you know the time?
   B: Yeah. It's half past six.

7. A: Pardon me. What time is it, please?
   B: Let's see here . . . It's a quarter to five.

8. **A:** Excuse me. Do you have the time, please?
   B: Sure. It's eight o'clock.

UNIT 11, P. 72

6. Listen to Stan and complete the sentences.

1. Every morning I <u>leave home</u> at 8:15.
2. Every morning after breakfast, I <u>brush my teeth.</u>
3. On week nights, I always <u>go to sleep</u> at 10:30.
4. Every morning before breakfast, I <u>take a shower.</u>
5. Every night after dinner, I <u>watch TV.</u>
6. On Sundays, I always <u>get up</u> at 9:00.
7. I always <u>eat lunch</u> at noon.
8. Every morning I <u>eat breakfast</u> at 7:00.

UNIT 11, P. 74

9. Listen to the conversations and write the missing words. Then practice the conversations with a partner.

1. **Tom:** Hi, Ann.
   Ann: Hi, Tom. Hey. Is something wrong? Are you <u>tired</u>?
   Tom: I'm very tired. I work too much.
   Ann: When do you <u>leave</u> for work?
   Tom: <u>At 6:30.</u>
   Ann: When do you get home?
   Tom: <u>At 11:30.</u>
   Ann: Oh no. That's terrible!

2. **Sue:** Hi, Tony.
   Tony: Hi, Sue. Hey. Is something wrong? Are you <u>worried?</u>
   Sue: I'm very worried. I study hard but I don't understand my homework.
   Tony: When do you do your <u>homework?</u>
   Sue: I start at <u>8:00.</u>
   Tony: When do you finish?
   Sue: Sometimes <u>at 1:00.</u>
   Tony: Oh no. That's terrible!

UNIT 12, P. 76

3. Listen to May and complete the sentences.

1. On Fridays and Saturdays, I <u>go to bed</u> late.

2. I <u>drink tea</u> every morning.

3. Sometimes I <u>work</u> on Sundays.

4. Sometimes I <u>go to church</u> on Sundays.

5. I <u>come</u> to school by bus everyday.

6. I <u>play tennis</u> every Saturday.

7. On weekdays, I <u>get up</u> early.

8. I usually <u>stay home</u> on weekends.

UNIT 12, P. 79

9. Listen to Sue, Lee, and Maria talk about their jobs. Check *yes* or *no* in the boxes below.

1. **Sue:** Yes, I have a full-time job. I work 7 hours a day 6 days a week. But I don't have good hours. I go to work very early – at 4:00 in the morning. I don't have a lunch break. After work, I'm tired and hungry. But I have a good boss. She's nice. I work on weekends, and I stay home on Monday.

2. **Lee:** I don't have a full-time job. I have a part-time job. I work 4 hours a day 5 days a week. I have good hours. They're not too early and not too late. I don't have a lunch break. But I have a coffee break at noon. I have a good boss, and I'm very happy with my job. I work Monday to Friday. I stay home on weekends.

3. **Maria:** I have a full-time job. I work 8 hours a day 5 days a week. I have good hours. I work 4 hours in the morning. Then I have a lunch break at noon. I work 4 more hours in the afternoon. I work Monday to Friday, and I don't work on weekends. But I don't have a good boss. He's not very nice. He's angry all the time.

   Boss: Maria! Where are you? What are you doing? Why aren't you at your desk!

   Maria: That's my boss. Coming, Mr. Morgan!

UNIT 13, P. 85

7. Listen to the telephone conversations. Write the missing information.

1. **A:** City Bus. Can I help you?
   B: Yes. I'm at the beach. I'm going downtown. What bus do I take?
   A: Take the #7.
   B: Where do I get on?
   A: At Polk and 2nd.
   B: Polk and 2nd. Where do I get off?
   A: At 42nd Street.
   B: 42nd Street. How much is the fare?
   A: 80 cents.
   B: Thank you.
   A: You're welcome. Goodbye.

2. **A:** City Bus. Can I help you?
   B: Yes. I'm at Mercy Hospital. I'm going downtown. What bus do I take?
   A: Take the #21.
   B: Where do I get on?
   A: At Post and 10th.
   B: Post and 10th. Where do I get off?
   A: At Park Street.
   B: Park Street. How much is the fare?
   A: $1.25.
   B: Thank you.
   A: You're welcome. Goodbye.

3. **A:** City Bus. Can I help you?
   B: Yes. I'm at the public library. I'm going downtown. What bus do I take?
   A: Take the #15.
   B: Where do I get on?
   A: At Holly and 47th.
   B: Holly and 47th. Where do I get off?

A: At 16th Street.
B: 16th Street. How much is the fare?
A: 75 cents.
B: Thank you.
A: You're welcome. Goodbye.

4. A: City Bus. Can I help you?
B: Yes. I'm at the police station.
I'm going downtown. I'm in a hurry.
What bus do I take?
A: Take the #1.
B: Where do I get on?
A: At Oak and 43rd.
B: Oak and 43rd. Where do I get off?
A: At 5th Street.
B: 5th Street. How much is the fare?
A: $1.15.
A: Hey, wait!
B: What's wrong, sir?
A: There goes the #1 bus! What am I
going to do now?
B: The next bus comes in 45 minutes.
A: I have to wait 45 minutes? Oh, no!

UNIT 14, P. 90

5. Listen to the conversations. Circle yes or no and write how much is in the account.

1. A: Can I help you?
B: Yes. Can you please cash this check?
A: Do you have an account with our bank?
B: Yes, I do.
A: All right. Please sign your name on the back of the check.
B: OK. And how much money do I have in my account?
A: You have $625.
B: Thank you.

2. A: Can I help you?
B: Yes. Can you please cash this check?
A: Do you have an account with our bank?
B: Oh yes. I come here all the time.
A: All right. Please sign your name on the back of the check.
B: OK. And how much money do I have in my account?
A: You have $1,000.
B: Thank you.

3. A: Can I help you?
B: Yes. Can you please cash this check?
A: Do you have an account with our bank?
B: No, I don't.
A: Where do you keep your money?
B: At First Bank. But First Bank is closed now.
A: Closed? At 4:30?
B: Yes. It closes at 4:00.
A: Well, all right. Please sign your name on the back of the check.
B: OK. Thank you.

4. A: Can I help you?
B: Yes. Can you please cash this check?
A: Do you have an account with our bank?
A: Yes, I do.
B: All right. Please sign your name on the back of the check.
A: OK. And how much money do I have in my account?
B: You have $975.
A: Thank you.

5. A: Can I help you?
B: Yes. Can you please cash this check?
A: Do you have an account with our bank?
B: No, I don't.
A: Where do you keep your money?
B: At First Bank.
A: First Bank is four blocks from here.
B: Four blocks? Look. The bank is closing now, and I'm tired.
A: I'm sorry, Miss Sanders. Five hundred dollars is a lot of money, and you don't have an account.
B: Can you . . .
A: First Bank is only four blocks away.
B: . . . please cash this check?
A: I'm sorry, but we can't.
B: Oh, all right!

UNIT 14, P. 91

7. Listen. Draw the hands on the clocks.

1. A: Do you have the time, please?
B: Yes. It's 8:10.
A: Did you say 8:10?
B: That's right.

2. A: Do you have the time?
B: Sure do. It's 12:55.
A: Was that 12:55?
B: Um hum.

3. A: What time is it, please?
B: Let's see . . . It's twenty past nine.
A: Twenty past nine?
B: Yup.

4. A: Excuse me. Do you have the time?
B: It's ten to three.
A: Did you say ten to three?
B: That's right.

5. A: Excuse me. Do you know what time it is?
B: Um hum. It's twenty-five after two.
A: Was that twenty-five after two?
B: That's right.

6. A: Excuse me. What time is it, please?
B: It's five minutes before eight.
A: Did you say five minutes before eight?
B: Um hum.

7. A: Can you tell me the time, please?
B: Sure can. It's five past twelve.

A: Five past twelve?
B: That's right.

8. A: Excuse me. Do you have the time, please?
B: Let's see here . . . It's twenty to eight.
A: Was that twenty to eight?
B: Yup.

UNIT 14, P. 92

8. Repeat the names of the places after your teacher. Then listen and write the opening and closing times in the boxes.

1. A: Public Library. May I help you?
B: Yes. What time do you open today?
A: We open at 9:00.
B: 9:00. And what time do you close?
A: We close at 5:00.
B: 5:00. One more question. Are you open on weekends?
A: On Saturday, we open at 12:00 and close at 5:00. But on Sundays, we're closed.
B: OK. Thanks for the information.
A: You're welcome. Goodbye.

2. A: Lane's Department Store. May I help you?
B: Yes. What time do you open today?
A: We open at 10:00.
B: 10:00. And what time do you close?
A: We close at 6:00.
B: 6:00. One more question. Are you open on weekends?
A: On Saturday, we open at 10:00 and close at 6:00.
B: Open at 10, close at 6:00.
A: On Sunday, we open at noon and close at 5:00.
B: Close at 6:00?
A: No, we close at 5:00.
B: OK. Thanks for the information.
A: You're welcome. Goodbye.

3. A: First National Bank. May I help you?
B: Yes. What time do you open today?
A: At 9:00.
B: 9:00. And what time do you close?
A: At 4:00.
B: 4:00. One more question. Are you open on Saturdays?
A: Yes. On Saturday, we open at 9:00 and close at 1:00. But we're closed on Sundays.
B: OK. Thanks for the information.
A: You're welcome. Goodbye.

4. A: Al's Barber Shop. Can I help you?
B: Yes. I'm coming in for a haircut now. OK?
A: I'm sorry, sir. We're closed now.
B: Closed? Oh no. My girlfriend is coming tonight!
A: We open at 9:30, and we close at 6:30 every day, sir. Come in tomorrow.
B: Tomorrow? Tomorrow's too late!
A: I'm very sorry, sir. The barber shop is closed now. Goodbye.
B: My girlfriend is coming and my hair is too long. This is terrible!

UNIT 16, P. 100

3. Listen to May and complete the sentences.

1. Most mornings I _get to work_ at about 8:00.

2. Most days I _relax_ after work.

3. Every day I _start work_ at 8:00.

4. Most nights I _watch TV_ before I go to sleep.

5. I always _catch the bus_ in front of my house.

6. Most evenings I _read the paper_ after dinner.

7. Every morning I _take a coffee break_ at work.

8. Every day I _finish work_ at 4:30.

UNIT 16, P. 104

9. Listen to Maria talk about her weekly schedule. Write the missing information.

I have a full-time job. Monday to Friday, I do the same thing every day. I start work at 8:00 in the morning and work until noon. I have a lunch break at 12:00. Then I work from 1:00 to 5:00 P.M.

After work, I'm tired, so I usually go home. I eat dinner at 6:00. Then I relax. I read the newspaper and watch TV until 10:00.

On Saturdays, I do a lot of things. First, I go to the bank at 9:00 in the morning. Then I take the bus downtown and go shopping until noon. I have a lot of fun. At 2:00 in the afternoon, I play tennis with a friend. We play for two hours. Saturday night, I go out with Stan. We usually watch a movie.

On Sunday mornings, I go to church from 10:00 to 12:00. Then I eat lunch. I usually eat in a restaurant. After lunch, I do my laundry. Later in the afternoon at about 3:00, I clean my apartment. Then, I'm very tired. So at night, I relax. After dinner, I write letters to my family and friends.

UNIT 17, P 106

3. Listen and complete the sentences.

1. I always _go dancing_ on Friday.

2. My sister usually _plays cards_ on Sunday.

3. My wife and I never _take a vacation_ .

4. I sometimes _go fishing_ in the summer.

5. My children usually _see a movie_ on Saturday.

6. I usually don't _eat out_ because it's expensive!

7. My parents sometimes _go bowling_ on the weekend.

8. My family _goes to church_ on Sunday.

UNIT 17, P. 110

10. Listen to Pablo, Sue, Jane, and Matt. Put a check above their sports and leisure activities.

1. My name is Pablo. I have leisure time at night and on the weekends. And I like sports. I play soccer with my friends. We play every Saturday morning, sometimes until 1:30 or 2:00 in the afternoon. We exercise a lot. I like fishing too. I go fishing with my brother about once a month. We go early in the morning and fish all day.

2. Hi. I'm Sue. I'm a student, so I don't have much leisure time. I take a lot of classes and I study hard. But I like sports. I play volleyball with friends from school. We play twice a week, on Tuesday and Thursday night. We get a lot of exercise. I like tennis too. But I don't have much time for it. I play tennis maybe three times a year.

3. My name is Jane. Sports? Yes, I like sports. I exercise a lot in my leisure time. I go swimming three times a week. I swim on Monday, Wednesday, and Friday evening. On the weekends, sometimes I play basketball with my friends. We play about twice a month, usually on Sunday afternoons.

4. Hi. I'm Matt. Leisure time? Sports? I don't know. I don't have time for sports anymore. I never play baseball. I never play basketball. I never go fishing. I don't do anything. But wait a minute. I *do* have a sport. Every Sunday afternoon, I sit on the sofa and watch football on TV. And I drink soda. That's my sport: I watch football on TV. I get a lot of exercise drinking soda!

UNIT 18, P. 113

3. Listen. Write the number of each person under the correct picture.

Person 1. My name's Lee, and I'm a teacher. Every day I teach lessons to my students. I teach night classes, so I start work at seven o'clock in the evening.

Person 2. I'm Tom. I'm a janitor and I work very hard cleaning buildings every day. My hours are not very good. I start work at four-thirty every afternoon.

Person 3. My name is Eva, and I'm a seamstress. I sew clothes on a sewing machine. I only work half-days, because I take care of my children in the morning. My job starts at noon.

Person 4. I'm a bus driver, and my name is Nancy. I drive a bus in a big city. It's hard work. And I have to get up early every day because I start work at five-fifteen in the morning.

Person 5. My name is Les, and I'm a dentist. Every day I take care of people's teeth. I clean their teeth and I take care of problems they have in their mouth. I start work at ten o'clock every morning.

Person 6. I'm a fire fighter, and my name is Tony. I put out big fires in houses and buildings, and it's not an easy job! And my hours are not easy, either. I sleep during the day because I start work at midnight. You see, it's not easy!

Person 7. My name is Peter, and I'm a mechanic. I can tell you, I'm very good at fixing cars. Every morning I start working at eight-fifteen.

Person 8. I'm Joe, and I work for the post office. I'm a mail carrier, and maybe I deliver the mail to *your* house! I have to get up early because I start my job at five o'clock in the morning.

Person 9. My name is Sue, and I'm a police officer. My job is not easy, and sometimes I am afraid. But I feel good because I help many people. I start work at seven o'clock in the morning.

Listen again. Write the time each person starts work. Remember to write A.M. or P.M.

UNIT 18, P. 115

7. Listen to the four conversations and number the pictures 1, 2, 3, and 4.

1. A: 911 emergency.
   B: Hello. I need help. There's a fire in my kitchen.
   A: What's your name?
   B: John Phillips.
   A: What's your address?
   B: 257 Lake Avenue.
   A: What's the cross street?
   B: Baker.
   A: OK. A fire truck is on the way.
   B: Thank you.

2. A: 911 emergency.
   B: Hello. There's a stranger in my apartment building.
   A: What's your name?
   B: Maria Lopez.
   A: What's your address?
   B: 704 Main Street, Apartment 404.
   A: What's the cross street?
   B: Broadway.
   A: OK. A police officer is on the way.
   B: Thank you.

3. A: 911 emergency.
   B: Hello. This is Frank Morgan. There's a car accident on the corner near my house.
   A: Where is the accident?
   B: At the corner of Holly and Polk.
   A: OK Mr. Morgan. What's your address?
   B: 1054 Holly Street.
   A: OK. An ambulance is on the way.

4. A: John? Honey, get up!
   B: Huh? What's wrong?
   A: John! There's someone downstairs!
   B: Someone downstairs?
   B: Call 911.

C: 911 emergency.
A: Hello, police? There's a stranger in my house!
C: What's your name?
A: May Phillips.
C: What's your address?
A: 257 Lake Avenue.
C: What's the cross street?
A: Oh no. Honey?
B: I'm going downstairs.
C: Hello? Hello? What's wrong?
B: It's Zabu! He's in the kitchen! There's food everywhere!
C: What's going on there?
A: I'm sorry. No one's downstairs. It's only our dog.
C: Your dog?
A: Yes. I'm *very* sorry.
C: No problem.
A: Goodbye.

UNIT 18, P. 116

8. Listen to Maria again and complete the conversation.

A: 911 emergency.
B: Hello. There's a <u>stranger</u> in my apartment building.
A: What's your name?
B: Maria Lopez.
A: What's your address?
B: <u>704</u> Main <u>Street</u>, Apartment <u>404.</u>
A: What's the <u>cross street</u>?
B: Broadway.
A: OK. A <u>police officer</u> is on the way.
B: Thank you.

UNIT 19, P. 118

2. Listen to John talk about his family and write the missing words.

I come from a big family. I have three <u>sisters</u> and four brothers. My <u>parents</u> live just a few blocks away from my house. My grandparents also live in the neighborhood. My <u>grandfather</u> is very old, but he goes to work every day. And my <u>grandmother</u> goes dancing with my <u>uncle</u>. He's not married. He's single. My <u>wife</u>, May, comes from China, and she likes big families. We have three <u>children</u>, but Zabu also thinks he's one of our <u>family</u>!

UNIT 19, P. 121

7. Listen to the four conversations and number the pictures 1, 2, 3, and 4.

1. A: Can I help you?
   B: Yes. Can I have six aerograms, please?
   A: OK. Anything else?
   B: No, thanks.
   A: That's $2.70.
   B: $2.70. Here you are.
   A: Thank you.

2. A: Can I help you?
   B: Yes. This package is going to China, please.
   A: Airmail?
   B: Yes. Airmail.
   A: That's $4.20.
   B: $4.20.
   A: Anything else?
   B: No, thanks.
   A: Here's your change.
   B: Thank you.

3. A: Can I help you?
   B: Yes. Can I have a money order, please?
   A: For how much?
   B: $400.
   A: $400. Here you are. Print the names and addresses on both sides.
   B: OK. Thank you.

4. A: Can I help you?
   B: Yes. Can I have ten 50-cent stamps, please?
   A: OK. Anything else?
   B: No, thanks.
   A: That's $5.00.
   B: $5.00. Hey, wait a minute. These are 5-cent stamps, not *50*-cent stamps.
   A: They are? Oh. You're right. I'm very tired today.
   B: You are?
   A: Yes. I work too hard. Next person in line, please.
   B: Hey. Where are my 50-cent stamps?
   A: Oh, yes. Here they are . . .
   B: OK. Thank you.

Listen again. Write how much things cost.

UNIT 20, P. 127

7. John and his family are camping. Listen and draw a line from the person to the problem he or she has.

1. John: Why is Tim crying?
   May: He's cold. He has the chills.
   John: The chills? Poor Tim!

2. John: Why is Kate crying?
   May: She has a cut on her hand.
   John: A cut? Poor Kate!

3. John: Why is the baby crying?
   May: He has a burn on his finger.
   John: A burn? Poor Ben!

4. John: Why is Zabu crying?
May: He has a bee sting.
John: A bee sting? Where?
May: On his nose.
John: Poor Zabu!

UNIT 20, P. 128

8. Listen to the conversations and write the missing words.

1. **A:** I have a <u>cut</u> on my finger.
   B: A cut? You need a <u>bandaid</u>.
   A: Yeah. Can you please get me one?
   B: Sure.

2. **A:** I have a <u>bee sting</u> on my face.
   B: A bee sting? You need <u>cream</u>.
   A: Yeah. Can you please get me some?
   B: Sure.

UNIT 21, P. 131

5. May and the children aren't feeling well. Listen to the conversations and write the information.

1. **Nurse:** Hello. Dr. Brown's office.
   May: Hello. This is May Phillips. I'm not feeling well. I want an appointment with the doctor, please.
   Nurse: What's wrong?
   May: My head hurts.
   Nurse: Can you come at 9:00 on Wednesday?
   May: 9:00 on Wednesday? Sure.
   Nurse: OK. Goodbye.

2. **Nurse:** Hello. Dr. Brown's office.
   May: Hello. This is May Phillips. My son Tim isn't feeling well. I want an appointment with the doctor, please.
   Nurse: What's wrong?
   May: His throat hurts.
   Nurse: Can you come at 1:30 tomorrow afternoon?
   May: 1:30 on Tuesday? Sure.
   Nurse: OK. Goodbye.

3. **Nurse:** Hello. Dr. Brown's office.
   May: Hello. This is May Phillips. My daughter Kate isn't feeling well. I want an appointment with the doctor, please.
   Nurse: What's wrong?
   May: Her stomach hurts.
   Nurse: Can you come at 11:15 tomorrow morning?
   May: 11:15 on Thursday? Sure.
   Nurse: OK. Goodbye.

4. **Nurse:** Hello. Dr. Brown's office.
   John: Hello. This is John Phillips. My son Ben isn't feeling well. I want an appointment with the doctor, please.
   Nurse: What's wrong?
   John: His ear hurts.
   Nurse: Can you come at 1:00 this afternoon?
   John: Let me look at the calendar. 1:00? No.

Nurse: How about 2:45?
John: OK. Oh, wait. No, we can't come at 2:45.
Nurse: How about 4:00?
John: No . . . Oh! What day is today?
Nurse: Today is Saturday.
John: Today isn't Sunday?
Nurse: No, Mr. Phillips! Today is Saturday! Can you come at 1:00 this afternoon?
John: Of course. And I'm sorry . . .
Nurse: It's OK Mr. Phillips. Goodbye!

UNIT 21, P. 134

10. John is having a checkup. Listen to the doctor and write the number under the correct picture.

1. **Doctor:** OK, John, lie on your back.
   John: On my back?
   Doctor: That's right.

2. **Doctor:** OK, now lie on your stomach. .
   John: On my stomach, huh?
   Doctor: Yup.

3. **Doctor:** Next I want you to raise your arm.
   John: Which arm?
   Doctor: Your right arm. Raise your right arm.
   John: OK.

4. **Doctor:** Now drop that arm.
   John: Drop it?
   Doctor: Yeah.

5. **Doctor:** Now look at me and open wide.
   John: OK.
   Doctor: That's it. Keep your mouth wide open.

6. **Doctor:** Now say, "Ahhhh!"
   John: Ahhhh!
   Doctor: Again.
   John: Ahhhh!

7. **Doctor:** Now breathe in.
   John: Breathe in?
   Doctor: That's right.

8. **Doctor:** Now hold your breath.
   Doctor: Keep holding your breath now.

9. **Doctor:** OK, breathe out. .
   Doctor: Yes, you can breathe out now.
   John: Whew!

10. **Doctor:** Now take off your shirt.
    John: My undershirt too?
    Doctor: No. Just take off your shirt.
    John: Just a minute here.

11. **Doctor:** Now bend your arm.
    John: Pardon me?
    Doctor: I said, bend your arm.
    John: OK.

12. **Doctor:** Now straighten your arm.
    John: Straighten it?

Doctor: Yeah.
Doctor: Well, that's it. Everything seems
OK. See you next year.
John: Thanks, Doc.

UNIT 22, P. 137

3. Listen and complete the sentences.

1. Stan isn't feeling well. His stomach <u>hurts</u>.
2. Tony is sick. He has a <u>sore throat</u>.
3. Look at Jane's arm. She has a <u>rash</u>.
4. May isn't feeling well. She has a <u>headache</u>.
5. Tim's sleeping in bed. He has a <u>cold</u>.
6. Help Mrs. Morgan sit down. She feels <u>dizzy</u>.
7. Mr. Morgan is sick in bed. He has a <u>fever</u>.
8. John isn't feeling well. He has a <u>cough</u>.

UNIT 22, P. 140

10. People aren't feeling well at school. Listen to the conversations and draw a line from the person to the correct health problem. Then write the medicine.

1. John: I'm not feeling well.
   Maria: What's the problem?
   John: I have a cough.
   Maria: Why don't you take some cough syrup?
   John: Cough syrup? That's a good idea.

2. Maria: I'm not feeling well.
   Friend: What's the problem?
   Maria: I have diarrhea.
   Friend: Why don't you take some diarrhea medicine?
   Maria: Diarrhea medicine? That's a good idea.

3. Stan: I'm not feeling well.
   Maria: What's the problem?
   Stan: I have a stomachache.
   Maria: Why don't you take some antacid?
   Stan: Antacid? That's a good idea.

4. Mr. Morgan: I'm not feeling well.
   Maria: What's the problem?
   Mr. Morgan: I have a fever.
   Maria: Why don't you take some aspirin?
   Mr. Morgan: Aspirin? That's a good idea. Do you have some?
   Maria: Yes. Here.
   Mr. Morgan: Oh no . . . Now my stomach hurts!
   Maria: Your stomach?
   Mr. Morgan: Yes! I need a bathroom!

UNIT 23, P. 142

3. Listen and complete the sentences.

1. On July 19, Maria is going to <u>play tennis</u>.

2. On July 12, Maria is going to <u>fly to Alaska</u>.

3. On July 11, Maria is going to <u>pack</u> for her trip.

4. On July 13, Maria is going to <u>ride a horse</u>.

5. On July 14, Maria is going to <u>go fishing</u>.

6. On July 17 and 18, Maria is going to <u>climb a mountain</u>.

UNIT 23, P. 143

5. Listen and find the date on the calendar. Write the date.

1. What's the date tomorrow?
2. What's the date three days from now?
3. What's the date next Friday?
4. What's the date this Saturday?
5. What's the date a week from today?
6. What's the date the day after tomorrow?
7. What's the date in four days?
8. What's the date next Tuesday?
9. What's the date five days from today?
10. What's the date this Thursday?

UNIT 23, P. 145

8. Stan is going to see Maria tomorrow. Listen to him and number the pictures 1–5.

Stan: Maria is on vacation now. But tomorrow, she's going to come home. I'm going to see her tomorrow evening. I'm so happy! Here's what I'm going to do before she comes.

First, I'm going to wash my hair. Maria really likes clean hair. Second, I'm going to dry my hair. That takes only a few minutes. Third, I'm going to comb my hair. I want it to look good.

After I finish my hair, I'm going to shave. I'm going to be very careful when I shave. I don't want to cut my face. Last, I'm going to brush my teeth. I want clean teeth, of course.

Then, I'll be ready to see Maria!

Stan: Who is it?

Maria: It's me. Maria.

Stan: What? Maria? But today is Saturday. You're coming home on Sunday!

Maria: I'm home a day early!

Stan: Early? But what about my hair? What about my face? What about my teeth? Oh no!

Maria: Come on Stan. Aren't you going to open the door?

UNIT 24, P. 149

3. Listen and complete the sentences.

1. On Tuesday, Maria is going to <u>get married</u>.

2. On Wednesday, the kids are going to <u>get in trouble</u>.

3. On Monday, Zabu is going to <u>eat all day</u>.

4. On Wednesday, John isn't going to <u>take the bus</u> .

5. On Tuesday, the kids aren't going to <u>clean their room</u> .

6. On Wednesday, Maria isn't going to <u>go to work</u> .

7. On Tuesday, Zabu isn't going to <u>do anything</u> .

8. On Monday, John is going to <u>get a raise</u> .

UNIT 24, P. 151

8. Listen to the conversations. Check leave early or day off and the correct day.

1. A: Can I leave work at 12:00 on Saturday?
   B: Why?
   A: My sister is going to get married.
   B: I'm sorry, but you can't leave early on Saturday. We're going to be too busy.
   A: Oh well.

2. A: Can I have the day off on Wednesday?
   B: Why?
   A: My wife isn't feeling well. She's going to go into the hospital.
   B: O K.
   A: Thank you.

3. A: Can I have the day off on Monday?
   B: Why?
   A: We're going to go camping this weekend. We want to stay three days.
   B: I'm sorry, but you can't have Monday off. We're going to be too busy.
   A: Oh well.

4. A: Can I leave work at 4:00 on Thursday?
   B: Why?
   A: My husband is coming home from Alaska. I'm going to meet him at the airport.
   B: O K.
   A: Thank you.

5. A: Can I have the day off on Friday?
   B: I'm sorry, but you can't. We're going to be too busy.
   A: But I'm going to get married on Friday!
   B: Married? But you don't have a girlfriend!
   A: Yes, I do!
   B: Since when?
   A: Since last weekend.
   B: And you're going to get married on Friday?
   A: Yes. Please give me the day off!
   B: Well, all right . . .
   A: All right! Thank you!
   B: Oh no. I can see it now. He's going to have *big* problems . . .

UNIT 25, P. 155

3. Listen and complete the sentences.

1. I can't <u>understand</u> these directions.

2. I can <u>explain</u> them for you.

3. I can't move this desk. It's <u>too heavy</u> .

4. I can <u>help you</u> move it.

5. I <u>can't</u> open this window.

6. <u>I'll open</u> it for you.

UNIT 25, P. 157

8. Look at the schedule changes with your teacher. Then listen to the conversations. Draw a line from the person to the schedule change. Then check *yes* or *no*.

1. Boss: Pablo, can you work the day shift next Monday?
   Pablo: Sure. No problem.

2. Boss: Nancy, can you work this weekend?
   Nancy: Sure. No problem.

3. Boss: Ann, can you work the night shift tomorrow?
   Ann: I'm sorry, but I can't. I'm visiting my father in the hospital.
   Boss: All right.

4. Boss: Peter, can you work overtime today?
   Peter: I'm sorry, but I can't. I'm taking my kids home from school.
   Boss: All right.

5. Boss: Matt, can you come in early tomorrow?
   Matt: Sure. What time?
   Boss: 5:30.
   Matt: 5:30! That's too early!
   Boss: Come at 6:30, then.
   Matt: 6:30! That's too early!
   Boss: What time *can* you come in?
   Matt: Ummmm. Around 8:00, I think.
   Boss: 8:00? That's when you usually come in!
   Matt: It is? Well I'm sorry, Mr. White. I guess I can't come in early. I have to sleep eight hours every night.
   Boss: Oh, all right!

UNIT 25, P. 158

9. Listen to the conversations and write the missing words.

1. A: Can you work the <u>day shift</u> next Saturday?
   B: Sure. No problem.

2. A: Can you <u>come</u> in <u>early</u> tomorrow?
   B: I'm sorry, but I can't. I'm <u>going</u> to the dentist at 11:00.
   A: All right.

3. A: Can you work <u>overtime</u> tonight?
   B: I'm sorry, <u>but I can't</u>. I'm meeting my sister at the airport tonight.
   A: All right.

Unit 26, p. 160

3. Listen and find the date on the calendar. Write the date below.

1. What was the date last Tuesday?
2. What was the date the day before yesterday?
3. What was the date two weeks ago on Thursday?
4. What was the date five days ago?
5. What was the date last Friday?
6. What was the date on Monday?
7. What's the date next Monday?
8. What's the date the day after tomorrow?
9. What's the date three days from now?
10. What's the date one week from today?

UNIT 26, P. 161

5. Listen and fill in the blanks.

1. Where did Maria go __yesterday__? To a restaurant.
2. Where did Maria go __three days ago__? To the hospital.
3. Where did Maria go __five days ago__? To the zoo.
4. Where did Maria go __last Friday__? To a party.
5. Where did Maria go __last Thursday__? To the hair salon.
6. Where did Maria go __the day before yesterday__? To the bank.
7. Where did Maria go __on Sunday__? To the park.

UNIT 27, P. 167

4. Listen and complete the sentences.

1. Last Thursday, May __danced__ all night.
2. Last Tuesday, John __coughed__ all day.
3. Last Tuesday, Zabu __played__ with the kids.
4. Maria and Stan __argued__ last Tuesday.
5. Last Wednesday, Maria and Stan __cried__ because they argued.
6. John __called in sick__ last Wednesday.
7. John __stayed home__ last Thursday.
8. Last Thursday, Zabu __didn't do anything__ all day long.

UNIT 27, P. 169

7. Listen to the other people call in sick. Put a check above their problem. Then circle yes, no, or maybe.

1. **Sam:** Sam's Grocery Store. Sam speaking.
   Mark: Hello, Sam. This is Mark Lane. I can't come to work today. I'm sick.

Sam: That's too bad. What's the problem?
Mark: I have a sore throat.
Sam: Oh. Are you coming back tomorrow?
Mark: I don't know. Maybe.
Sam: OK. I hope you feel better.
Mark: Thanks. Goodbye.

2. **Mr. D:** Mr. D's Restaurant. Mr. D. speaking.
   Peter: Hello, Mr. D. This is Peter. I can't come to work today. I'm sick.
   Mr. D: That's too bad. What's the problem?
   Peter: I have a toothache.
   Mr. D: Oh. Are you coming back tomorrow?
   Peter: Yes. I'm going to see the dentist today.
   Mr. D: OK. I hope you feel better.
   Peter: Thanks. Goodbye.

3. **Joe:** Joe's Auto Garage. Joe speaking.
   Sam: Hello, Joe. This is Sam. I can't come to work today. I'm sick.
   Joe: That's too bad. What's the problem?
   Sam: I have a cold.
   Joe: Oh. Are you coming back tomorrow?
   Sam: No, I don't think so. I'm feeling bad.
   Joe: OK. I hope you feel better.
   Sam: Thanks. Goodbye.

4. **Mrs. Lo:** Sewing Shop. Mrs. Lo speaking.
   Eva: Hello, Mrs. Lo. This is Eva Garcia. I can't come to work today. I'm sick.
   Mrs. Lo: Oh. That's too bad. What's the problem?
   Eva: I have a backache.
   Mrs. Lo: Oh. Are you coming back tomorrow?
   Eva: I don't know. Maybe.
   Mrs. Lo: OK. I hope you feel better.
   Eva: Thanks. Goodbye.

5. **Mr. Morgan:** English Language School. Mr. Morgan speaking.
   Stan: Hello, Mr. Morgan. This is Stan Hill. I can't come to work today. I'm sick.
   Mr. Morgan: That's too bad. What's the problem?
   Stan: I think I have the flu.
   Mr. Morgan: Oh. Are you coming back tomorrow?
   Stan: Ohhh!
   Mr. Morgan: What's the matter? Are you there, Stan? What's wrong?
   Stan: I feel dizzy . . .
   Mr. Morgan: All right, Stan. Go to bed right now, and stay home tomorrow, too.
   Stan: OK, Mr. Morgan.
   Mr. Morgan: I hope you feel better.
   Stan: Me too. Goodbye.

Teacher's Notes

BEFORE UNIT 1

Reinforce the vocabulary from page 1 as follows:

1. Have students *pantomime* responses to your commands: "**Listen to** your watch/me/the cars outside." **Look at** the clock/ the chalkboard/your watch." **Write on** your paper/ the chalkboard/your desk." "**Read** the newspaper/your book/your neighbor's book."

2. Write the words *name, day, time,* and *age* on the chalkboard and, pointing to one at a time, instruct students to "**ask the question**" or "**answer the question.**"

3. Say one of the following cues: "*1, 2, 3...,*" "*A, B, C...*" or "*Mon., Tues., Wed...*"followed by one of the instructions "**Repeat,**" "**Continue,**" "**Go on,**" or "**Next,**" and have students respond appropriately.

Reinforce the vocabulary from page 3 as follows:

1. Write three simple sentences on the board and, as you point to individual words or sentences, ask, "How many **vowels/words/sentences/letters?**", "Whats the first/last **word/sentence/letter/vowel?**"

2. Write the words *up, small, fast, sad,* and *open* on the chalkboard and, pointing to one at a time, ask students, "What does this **mean?**", "How do you **say** this?" "How do you **spell** this?" and "What's the **opposite?**" (Students can give the meanings by pantomime, paraphrasing, etc.)

UNITS 1-27

Please read Presenting New Vocabulary with Pictures (page viii) before reading the following notes.

This section includes, for Units 1-27, questions to ask while presenting the pictures on the first page, and a sample of how the presentation of the page might start out. Since actual classroom presentations will be interactive, and therefore guided by students' responses, they will not follow these models exactly. That is, these are not scripts, but rather guides from which to draw ideas for creating natural and personalized presentations suited to your students.

Specific teaching notes are also given for selected units. You are urged to read these notes before beginning a new unit, although with time you may find it unnecessary to refer to the sample presentations.

UNIT 1: **What's Your First Name? (page 9)**

Teaching note: Look at page 10 to present the pictures (vocabulary) on page 9. (The students will be looking at page 9.) Ask the questions that appear next to the pictures. First ask each question about Maria (whose answers are given on page 9), and then ask the questions of several students, who will give their own answers.

Sample presentation, Picture 9: first/last/full name

Today we're going to talk about personal information. Personal information is your name, how old you are and what else? . . . Your telephone number. And what else? Your address. . . . Those things are all personal information. Let's start with this picture. Do you remember who this is? . . . It's Maria. And what's this [pointing to her name tag]? . . . Yes, it's her name. Now, what is her *first* name? . . . Good, her first name is Maria. And her *last* name? . . . Yes, it's Lopez. Well, then, what's her *full* name? . . . Right, her full name is Maria Lopez. So what does "full name" mean? . . . Yes, your full name is your first name *and* your last name. Now [looking at a student], what's *your* last name? . . . Chen? OK. And your first name? . . . Bao Ping? Yes. So, class, what's his full name? . . . His full name is Bao Ping Chen.

UNIT 2: **Where's John? (page 17)**

Ask questions like the following to present the pictures:

• Where's this person? *or* What (place) is this?
• Is there a (park) near your house?
  or Is there a (park) in our city? (Where is it?)
• What do we do at a (park)?
• When do we go to a (park)?
• Are you inside or outside when you're at a (park)?

The Pictures

1. store	5. airport	9. party
2. hospital	6. beach	10. home
3. movie theater	7. zoo	11. school
4. bus stop	8. park	12. work

Sample presentation, Picture 1: at the store

Today, we're going to talk about places. First, let's see where John is. See John's name here? Is he at home or is he at the store? . . . Yes, he's at the store. Now, what do you do at a store? . . . You buy food at a store. And what else? . . . Yes, you buy clothes at a store. Are there any stores near your house? . . . There's a drug store near your house, José? Anybody else? . . . There's a supermarket near your house, Mei. Yes, a supermarket is a store. And where are there *lots* of stores? . . . OK, on Main Street. Now take a look at this word [pointing to "sale" in the picture]—it says "sale." Do you know what a sale is? . . . Well, do you have a sale at a store or at school? . . . Yes, you have a sale at a store. And what is a sale? . . . OK, a sale means a cheap price. Is a sale an everyday price? . . . No, it's a special, cheap price. So where is John? . . . At the store. And the store is having a sale.

UNIT 3: **What Size Is the Shirt? (page 23)**

Ask questions like the following to present the pictures:

• What (item of clothing) is this?
• How much is this (shirt)?
• What size is this (shirt)?
• Where (on your body) do you put a (shirt)?
• Who in this class is wearing a (shirt)?
• What color is his/her (shirt)?

The Pictures

1. shirt—$19, Large	4. sweater—$24.99, Large
2. blouse—$12, Small	5. belts—$3.99, 34 inches
3. skirt—$18, Medium	6. ties—two for $8

7. shoes—$29.99, size 9 ½
8. socks—$3.50, size 10
9. pants—$15, size 32/31
10. T-shirt—$6, Extra Large
11. hat—$8.95, Medium

12. coat—$60, Large
13. jacket—$39, Medium
14 gloves—$4.99, Small
15. dress—$22, Petite
16. underwear—$2.99

Sample presentation, Picture 1: a shirt

Today we're going to talk about clothes—you know [pointing], shirt, pants, socks: clothes. What's this? Is it a pair of pants? . . . No. Is it a shirt? . . . Yes, it's a shirt. Let's see now, who has a shirt on in this class? . . . Yes, you have a shirt on, Ali. What color is Ali's shirt? . . . Ali's shirt is blue. Who else? . . . Yes, Maria has a shirt on. Is that a new shirt or an old one, Maria? . . . Oh, it's new. It looks new! Now, let's look at the *size* of this shirt. What size is it [pointing to the "L" in the picture]? . . . It's large. What does "large" mean? . . . Right, it means "big." Anybody here have a large shirt? . . . Paulo, your shirt size is large? So, class, what does "size" mean? . . . Yes, it means "big" or "small." Now, what about the *price* of this shirt? What price is it? . . . Right, it's $19 [pointing to the price in the picture]. What's the price of this book? . . . The price was $12. And the price of that pencil, Deng? . . . Oh, the price was 29 cents? . . .

UNIT 4: Where's Zabu? (page 29)

Teaching note: During the presentation and conversation practice in this unit, students will be asked a question whose answer is not given in the book—"Why is Zabu in this place?" Here, as in other places indicated in the book, the aim is to reinforce the new language—and have some fun—by engaging in free speculation.

For each picture on page 1, first ask the following two questions:

- Where's Zabu?
- What's he doing there? (free speculation)

Then elicit other visible illustrations of the preposition being taught, as in the sample presentation below.

The Pictures

1. inside/in his house
2. outside his house
3. in the corner
4. around his house
5. above/over his house
6. under/below his house
7. in front of his house
8. in back of/behind his house
9. on top of his house
10. at the corner (of the street)
11. next to/beside his house
12. between the houses

Sample presentation, Picture 1: inside his house

Let's see, who do we have here?...Yes, this is Zabu. And where is he, at home or in the park?...Yes, he's at home. This is his house. Now, is Zabu *inside* his house or *outside*

his house?...Yes, he's inside his house. "Inside" is the same meaning as... Yes, it's the same as "in." Now, what's Zabu doing inside his house? Any ideas?...Yes, he's just sitting there. *Why* is he sitting inside his house?...Yes, he looks sad. What is he thinking about? ... Maybe he's thinking about food. Now, what about *us*? Are we inside our houses?...No, we're inside the classroom. And what about my teeth [showing teeth]? They're inside my...yes, inside my mouth. And your money?...Yes; it's inside your purse.

Presenting page 33

Ask questions like the following for each of the items on the shelves and counter on page 33.

- What's this (called)? (What are these called?)
- What's it (used) for? (What are they used for?)
- Where (in the picture) is it? (Where are they?)

Sample presentation: dishes, knives, and fork

What kind of store is this, class? A drug store? . . . No, it's a department store. But what's all this [pointing]? It looks like a . . . yes, a kitchen. This woman is cooking food to show the customers. Now look at the things in this kitchen. What are these? . . . Yes, they're dishes. What are dishes for [pantomiming]? . . . For eating food. What color are the dishes in your house, Tam? . . . Your dishes are white. And yours, Yukiko? . . . Blue. Now, *where* are the dishes—on the floor or on the counter? . . . Yes, they're on the counter. Do you have a counter in your house, Juan? . . . In the kitchen. OK. And are there counters in stores? . . . Yes, there are. So, these two dishes are on the counter. And what's this? . . . Right, it's a knife. What's a knife for [pantomiming]? . . . For cutting. And where is this knife? . . . Yes, it's *between* the dishes. What about these? . . . Yes, they're forks. Do you use forks in China, Jimmy? . . . Not very much. And where are the forks? . . . Yes, they're *on top of* the dishes . . .

UNIT 5: What's John Doing? (page 35)

Ask questions like the following to present the pictures:

- Where's this person? *or* What place is this? (review)
- What's s/he doing?
- Is s/he (sleeping) or (swimming)?
- When do we (swim)?
- Where do we (swim)?
- Do you ever (swim)?
- Do you like to (swim)?

The Pictures

1. school—teach a lesson
2. home—sleep
3. theater—watch a movie
4. bus stop—wait for the bus
5. airport—meet a friend
6. beach—swim

7. hospital—visit a friend
8. park—run
9. store—buy food
10. zoo—look at animals
11. work—drive a truck
12. party—dance

Sample presentation, Picture 1: teach a lesson

Today we're going to talk about what people are *doing*. For example, what are *you* doing? Are you eating, or are you studying? . . . You're studying. Now let's see what some other people are doing. First, we have John again. Do you remember where John is in this picture? . . . Yes, he's at school. And what's he doing? Is he studying? . . . No, he's not studying. Well, then, is he eating dinner or is he teaching a lesson? . . . Yes, he's teaching a lesson. Now, who's teaching a lesson in our class? Are you teaching a lesson? . . . No, you're studying. So who's teaching a lesson? . . . Yes, *I'm* teaching a lesson. Is this an English lesson or a cooking lesson? . . . It's an English lesson. And what lesson am I teaching [pointing to few of the pictures]? Is it a lesson about clothes? . . . No, it isn't a lesson about clothes. What lesson am I teaching? It's a lesson about . . . Yes, a lesson about places.

UNIT 6: Who's Cleaning the House? (page 41)

Ask questions like the following to present the pictures:

• What's this person doing?
• Is s/he (cleaning) or (sleeping)?
• When do we (clean)?
• Where do we (clean)?
• Why do we (clean)? *or* Why is s/he (cleaning)?
• Do you like to (clean)?

The Pictures

1. clean the house
2. sleep
3. wash the dishes
4. cook a meal
5. fill out a form
6. write a letter
7. get dressed
8. get undressed
9. drink coffee
10. take a shower
11. take a bath
12. not do anything

Sample presentation, Picture 1: clean the house

Today we're going to talk about what people are doing. Who's in this picture? . . . Yes, it's John. And what's he doing here? Is he teaching a lesson in this picture? . . . No, he's not teaching a lesson. So what's he doing? . . . Yes, he's cleaning. And what is he cleaning—his school or his house? . . . Yes, he's cleaning his house. Now what about you, Phuong, do you clean your house sometimes?

. . . Yes, you do? And do you *like* to clean your house? . . . No, you don't like to clean your house. Me neither! I don't like to clean my house. When do you usually clean your house, Phuong? At night? On the weekends? . . . Oh, you usually clean your house on Sunday. What about you, Leticia? When do you clean your house? . . . What? You don't clean your house?. . . Oh, I see. Your *husband* cleans your house. Lucky you!

UNIT 7: Why Is John Crying? (page 45)

Ask questions like the following to present the pictures:

• What's this person doing?
• Why is s/he (crying)?
• How is s/he feeling?
• Do you ever (cry)?
• Why do people (cry)?
• When do you feel (sad)?
• What do *you* do when you feel (sad)?

The Pictures

1. John crying—sad
2. Kim and Tate arguing—angry
3. Baby Ben yawning—tired
4. May biting her nails—worried
5. Maria scratching her head—confused
6. Zabu barking—scared

Sample presentation, Picture 1: John crying

Today we're going to talk about *feelings*. Do you know feelings? For example, how am I feeling now [making a happy face]? . . . Yes, I'm feeling happy. And how am I feeling now [making a sad face]? . . . Yes, I'm feeling sad. What are some other feelings? . . . Yes, *tired* [acting tired], and . . . *cold* [cold]. These are *feelings*. Well, now, what do we have here? Is this a pencil or a photo? . . . Yes, it's a photo. Do any of you have photos with you? Do you have a photo of your children, anyone? . . . Oh, nice, José! What a nice photo of your little girl. Now let's look at this photo here . Who is this? . . . It's our old friend, John. But look! What's he doing? Is he smiling? . . . No, he's not smiling . . . Yes, he's crying. Poor John! Now, who else cries? I mean, who cries *a lot*? . . . Yes, babies cry a lot. Babies cry when they're . . . Yes. Babies cry when they're hungry. And when do we cry, when we're happy or when we're sad? Yes, when we're sad. And when are we sad? . . . OK, we're sad when we lose a job. When else are we sad? . . . Yes, we're sad when our friend goes away. So what's John doing? . . . Yes, he's crying. And why is he crying? . . . Yes, because he's sad.

UNIT 8: What's Maria Doing Tomorrow? (page 49)

Teaching note: This unit is atypical in that students will be producing statements just after you have presented the vocabulary, as in the sample presentation. Allow several students to produce each of the statements, and allow extra time for this presentation.

Ask these questions about Maria's day:

1. What's Maria doing?
2. Where's she playing baseball?
3. Who's she playing baseball with?
4. When's she playing baseball?
5. How's she getting to the park?

Answers

1. Playing baseball.
2. In the park.
3. Her mother.
4. In the morning.
5. By bus.

Ask these questions about Stan's day:

1. What's Stan doing?
2. Where's he doing his laundry?
3. How's he getting there?

Answers

1. (He's doing) his laundry.
2. At the laundromat.
3. By car. *or* He's driving.

Ask these questions about John's day:

1. What's John doing?
2. Who's he fixing his car with?
3. Where's he fixing his car?
4. When's he fixing his car?

Answers

1. Fixing his car.
2. His father.
3. In the garage.
4. In the afternoon.

Ask this question about Zabu's day:

What's Zabu doing?

Answer

Nothing. *or* He's not doing anything.

Ask these questions about Tim and Kate's day:

1. What are Tim and Kate doing?
2. Where are they studying?
3. Who are they studying with?
4. When are they studying?

Answers

1. Studying.
2. At school.

3. Their classmates.
4. All day.

Ask these questions about Mr. and Mrs. Morgan's day:

1. What are Mr. and Mrs. Morgan doing?
2. Where are they going fishing?
3. Who are they going with?
4. How are they getting to the beach?

Answers

1. (Going) fishing.
2. At the beach.
3. Their dog.
4. They're walking.

Sample presentation, Picture 1: Maria's day

Let's see what Maria is doing tomorrow. Is she going to work, or playing baseball? . . . She's playing baseball. Anyone here play baseball? . . . Oh, Pedro, you play baseball. Good. How about you, Chau? . . . No? . . . Oh, they don't play much baseball in your country. I see. Now, *where* is Maria playing baseball [pointing to the trees]? . . . Yes, she's playing baseball in the park. And who is she playing with? Her father or her mother [pointing to the mother]? No question about this one; it's her mother. And *when* is she playing [pointing to the sun going up]? . . . Yes, in the morning. How did you know it was morning, Kim? . . . Yes, because the sun is going up. Now, how is Maria getting to the park [pointing to the bus]? Is she walking? . . . No, she's taking the bus. Now look at the picture and listen. [Slowly, pointing to individual parts of the picture] Maria's playing baseball in the park with her mother in the morning. She's taking the bus there. Who can say that? . . . Tran, you want to try? Go ahead.

UNIT 9: Is There a Post Office in Your Neighborhood? (page 55)

Presenting page 55
Ask questions like the following to present the pictures on page 55:

- What is this (place)? *or* What are these?
- What do we do at a (post office)? *or* Where do you find (a mailbox)?
- Is/are there (a post office) near your house?
- How far is it from your house?
- Are there many (post offices) in our city?

The Pictures

1. post office	7. health clinic
2. trees	8. hills
3. mailbox	9. library
4. tall buildings	10. restaurants
5. day-care center	11. movie theater
6. parking meters	12. pay phones

Sample presentation, Picture 1: post office

Today we're going to talk about some more places in town. Let's take a look at this place. What is this? Does anybody know? . . . Well, what is this [pointing to the stamp]? . . . Yes, it's a stamp. So what is this place? . . . Yes, it's a post office. Now what do we do at the post office? Do we go dancing? . . . No. What do we do? . . . Yes, we buy stamps. Like this stamp [pointing]. What else do we do at the post office? . . . Yes, we send letters. What else? . . . Yes, we send packages at the post office. Now, is there a post office near school? . . . Yes, there's a post office on Maple Street. How far is it to walk to that post office? . . . Yes, it's about a five minutes' walk to the post office on Maple Street.

Presenting page 57

Ask questions like the following to present the pictures on page 57:

- What is this?
- Is this (a TV) or (a VCR)?
- Is/are there (a TV) in your house?
- Is/are there (a TV) in our school?
- Where do you put/find (a TV)?
- What do we use (a TV) for?

The Pictures

1. TV
2. VCR
3. plants
4. dishwasher
5. pictures
6. basement
7. stairs
8. garage
9. bookshelves
10. ghost
11. closets
12. mice

Sample presentation, Pictures 1 and 2 : TV and VCR

Today, we're going to talk about things in your house. What's this? . . . Yes, it's a television. Or, we can say . . . ? Yes, "TV" is the same as "television." I think everyone knows what a TV is. But what's this next thing? . . . Yes, we use it to watch videos, and what do we call it? . . . Well, is it a clock, or a VCR? . . . Yes, it's a VCR. And we use a VCR together with what? . . . Yes, we use a VCR with our TV. And what do we watch on a VCR? . . . Yes, we watch videos. Videos of what? . . . Yes, we watch movies on our VCR. And you say you watch your baby on the VCR, Ana? How nice! You make movies of your baby and watch them on the VCR. So, class, is there a VCR in Ana's house? . . . Yes, there is.

UNIT 10: **Where's the Bedroom? (Page 63)**

Teaching note: First introduce the names of the lettered rooms and areas, then proceed to the numbered

furnishings. Look at page 64 as you present the names of the furnishings.

Ask questions like the following to present the rooms and areas:

- What room is this?
- Is it upstairs or downstairs?
- What do we do in a (kitchen)?
- Do you have a (basement) in your house?
- What color is the (kitchen) in your house?
- Is the (bedroom) in your house upstairs or downstairs?

The Rooms and Areas

a. bedroom
b. hallway
c. bathroom
d. living room
e. kitchen
f. basement
g. yard
h. garage

Sample presentation: bedroom

What do we have here? . . . Yes, this is a house. Today we're going to talk about houses. And how many rooms are there in this house? . . . Yes, there are five rooms [pointing to them]. How many rooms are there in your house, Ali? . . . Three rooms? What about your house, Chris? . . . Two rooms? Now then, in this picture, which room is the bedroom? . . . Yes, room "a" is the bedroom. What do we do in a bedroom? Do we eat? . . . No, we sleep in a bedroom. What color is your bedroom, Yukiko? . . . Your bedroom is white? My bedroom is white, too. Is this bedroom downstairs or upstairs? Yes, it's upstairs. Well, then, where is the hallway? . . . Yes, it's "b" . . .

To review rooms and areas

What letter is the garage? . . . Yes, it's "h". And the kitchen? . . . Yes, the kitchen is "e" . . .

Look at page 64 as you present the furnishings, and ask questions like the following:

- What is this?
- Is this a (bed) or a (dresser)?
- Where do we find a (dresser)?
- What do we use a (dresser) for?
- Do you have a (dresser) in your house?
- Where is the (dresser) in your house?
- What color is the (dresser) in your house?

Sample presentation: dresser

Let's go back to the bedroom now and look inside. What's this? . . . Is it a bed or a dresser? . . . Yes, it's a dresser. Now what do we keep in a dresser? . . . Do we keep hamburgers? . . . No, we keep clothes in a dresser. Where is the dresser in this bedroom? . . . Yes, the dresser is next to the closet. Do you have a dresser in your bedroom, Bao Zhu? . . . You do? What about you, Amy? . . . You have a dresser too? What color is your dresser? . . . Your dresser is brown. And how big is your dresser? . . .

To review furnishings

Do you remember these things? Tell me, what number is the scale? . . . Yes, the scale is number 11 [pointing]. And what about the curtains? . . . Yes, the curtains are number 13 [pointing] . . .

UNIT 11: **What Time Is It, Please? (page 69)**

Teaching note: As you ask students when *they* do the various activities on page 71, if a student attempts a negative response, demonstrate the answer—"I don't_____" —and clarify the meaning, if necessary. For faster classes, suggest answers utilizing the time-related words from page 73 of the unit—"*at* 7:15," "*about* 6:00," "*before* work," and "*after* school"—before the formal presentation of these time expressions on that page.

Ask questions like the following to present the pictures on page 71:

• What is s/he doing in this picture?
• When do people (get up)?
• Do *you* (watch TV) every day?
• What time do you (get up)?
• Where do people (do homework)?
• Where do *you* (do homework)?

The Pictures

1. get up
2. take a shower
3. shave
4. eat breakfast
5. leave home
6. eat lunch
7. go home *or* return home
8. eat dinner
9. watch TV
10. do homework
11. brush your teeth
12. go to bed *or* go to sleep

Sample presentation, Picture 1: get up

Today we're going to talk about *what time* we do things every day. Let's look at this picture. Is this person getting up, or going to sleep [pointing to the sun]? . . . Yes, he's getting up. Now, when do we get up? Do we get up in the morning or at night? . . . Yes, we get up in the morning. And *where* do we get up? In the kitchen? . . . No! We get up in the bedroom. Now Jacques, when do *you* get up every day? . . . At five o'clock?! My goodness! And what about you, Gunther? When do you get up every morning? . . . At eight thirty? Now that's more like it!

UNIT 12: **Do You Work on Sundays? (page 75)**

Teaching note: Before beginning this presentation, write "Do you . . . ?" on the chalkboard, reminding the students that "do" questions refer to *usually*, *every day*, or *sometimes*. Then tell the class that the two answers to this question are "Yes, I do" and "No, I don't."

Ask questions like the following to present the pictures:

• Do you (drink tea)?
• Do you *like* (working on Sundays)?
• Do you (play tennis) every day/week?
• Do you *always* (tell the truth)?
• Does your wife/husband (drink tea)?
• Why do/don't you (get up early)?
• When/where do you (play tennis)?

The Pictures

1. work on Sundays
2. drink tea
3. take the bus to school *or* come to school by bus
4. stay home on weekends
5. go to bed late
6. go home after class
7. tell the truth
8. eat a lot of fish
9. sing in the shower
10. get up early
11. play tennis
12. go to church

Sample presentation, Picture 1: work on Sundays

Today we're going to talk about things that we do, and things we don't do. Let's take a look at this picture. What's this person doing? Is he eating, or is he working? . . . Yes, he's working. Now, what are these letters across the top of the picture [pointing]? . . . Let's see, seven letters, seven days of the week. Any ideas? . . . Yes: Sunday, Monday, Tuesday . . . And what day is this [pointing to the circled *S*]? . . . Yes, it's Sunday. Now tell me, Victor, do you work on Sundays? . . . No, you don't. What about you, Marja? Do you work on Sundays? . . . Yes, you do. *Every* Sunday? . . . Oh, just sometimes. And do you *like* working on Sundays? . . . You don't like it very much. I wouldn't like it either.

UNIT 13: **How Do You Get to Work? (page 81)**

Teaching note: Look at page 82 as you present page 81, asking students the target question that is given for each picture. As you ask these questions, help students with their responses, using the answers on page 83 as a guide. Write the highlighted frequency expressions from page 83 on the chalkboard as you progress through the presentation. Explain their meanings and leave them on the board for students to refer to as they answer your questions.

Sample presentation, Picture 1: How do you get to work?

Today we're going to talk some more about things we do. Shao Lin, *how* [pointing to the word by the picture] do you get to work? . . . Well, do you walk? Do you drive? Do you swim? . . . I see. You walk to work. And what about you, Tamim? How do you get to work? . . . By car. You drive to work. And you, Sho? How do you get to work? . . . You take the bus. And what about you Ursula? How do you get to work? . . .

UNIT 14: Where Do You Keep Your Money? (page 87)

Teaching note: When you ask what people do at the different stores, students' responses (during the presentation and during the conversation practice) needn't be restricted to those listed on page 88. The captions in the book are for students' reference, but can be varied or expanded on.

Ask questions like the following to present the pictures:

- What (place) is this?
- What do we do/buy at a (bank)?
- What's the name of *your* (bank)?
- How far is your (bank) from your house?
- Is there a (bank) near your house?
- Is there a (bank) near school?

The Pictures

1. bank—keep your money
2. drug store—buy medicine
3. barber shop *or* hair salon—get a haircut
4. supermarket *or* grocery store—buy food
5. department store—buy clothes
6. second hand store *or* thrift shop—buy used things
7. hardware store—buy tools
8. auto repair shop—fix your car
9. furniture store—buy chairs, beds, and other furniture
10. gas station—get gas
11. produce store—buy fruit and vegetables
12. parking lot—park your car

Sample presentation, Picture 1: bank

Today we're going to talk about stores and other places in town. First let's look at this place. What's this, do you think? It's a place with lots of money! . . . Yes. It's a bank. Now, what do you do at a bank? Do you keep your children at the bank? . . . No. Do you keep your car at the bank? . . . No again. Well, what do you keep at the bank? . . . Yes, you keep your money at the bank. Aziz, do you keep your money at the bank, or under your bed? . . . You keep it at the bank. And what bank do you keep *your* money at? . . . At First Bank. How far is First Bank from your house? Five minutes? Ten minutes? . . . I see. About a five minutes' walk.

UNIT 15: Where's the Supermarket? (page 93)

For each picture, ask:

- Where's the supermarket?

Then elicit familiar examples of the street location being taught, as in the sample presentation below.

The Pictures

1. on First Street
2. on Second Street between Park and Lake Avenue *or* in the middle of the block
3. on the corner of Third and Main
4. across from the hospital
5. next (door) to the drug store *or* beside the drug store

Sample presentation, Picture 1: on First Street

Today we're going to talk about locations. We're going to talk about where things are on the street. Look at this picture. Remember what kind of store this is [pointing]? . . . Yes, it's a supermarket. Now where is the supermarket? Is it on Green Street? . . . No. . . . Yes, it's on First Street. And what about our school? Where is our school? . . . Yes, it's on Filbert Street. Now what about your house, Yuk? Where's your house? . . . I see, it's on Stockton Street. And your house, Luis? . . .

UNIT 16: What Time Does May Leave Home? (page 99)

Ask questions like the following to present the pictures:

- What's May doing (in this picture)?
- Is she (leaving home) or (catching the bus)?
- When does she (catch the bus) every day?
- Do you (catch the bus) every day?
- What time do *you* usually (catch the bus)?
- Where do you usually (catch the bus)?

The Pictures

1. leave home
2. catch the bus
3. get to work
4. start work *or* begin work
5. take a coffee break
6. eat lunch
7. finish work *or* get off work
8. get home
9. relax
10. cook dinner
11. read the paper
12. watch TV

Sample presentation, Picture 1: leave home

Today we're going to talk about May's daily routine. Let's look at this picture. What's May doing? Is she watching TV, or is she leaving home? . . . Yes, she's leaving home. By the way, when do we leave home—at night? . . . No, we leave home in the morning. And what time does May leave home every morning [pointing to the clock]? . . . Yes, she leaves home at 7:25. What about you, Delma? What time do you leave home every morning? . . . I see, at half past eight. Not bad. And what about you, Mehmet? What time do you leave home? . . .

UNIT 17: How Often Do You Go Dancing? (page 105)

Teaching note: Before beginning this presentation, write "How often?" on the chalkboard and establish its meaning with a few simple examples, such as, "How often do you go to work? . . . Every day." "How often do you brush your teeth? . . . Two times a day." Then underline the question and below it write the expressions of frequency that appear on page 107, introducing and clarifying them one by one. Elicit examples of each expression in relation to familiar activities and leave the expressions on the chalkboard to prompt students during the presentation.

Ask questions like the following to present the pictures:

- What's this person doing?
- Do you ever (go dancing)?
- How often do you (go dancing)?
- Where do you usually (go dancing)?
- What day do you (go dancing)?
- Who do you (go dancing) with?

The Pictures

1. go dancing
2. play cards
3. go fishing
4. watch a movie
5. go swimming
6. exercise
7. eat out
8. take a nap
9. take a vacation
10. go bowling
11. go to church
12. kiss your husband/wife

Sample presentation, Picture 1: go dancing

Now we're going to talk about things we do in our leisure time. What's "leisure time"? . . . Well, we have leisure time on Sunday, or after work. . . . Yes. Leisure time is free time. Now look at this picture. What's this person doing? . . . Yes, she's dancing. Fanny, how often do you go dancing? . . . Every Saturday and Sunday? Wow, that's great! Where do you usually go dancing? . . . Oh, at Disco-Land. What about you, Kim, how often do you go dancing? . . . Not very much. And how about you, Gabriela, how often do you go dancing? . . .

UNIT 18: What Does Sue Do? (page 111)

Teaching note: When you ask what the various people do in their jobs, students' responses (during the presentation and during conversation practice) needn't be restricted to those listed on page 112. The captions in the book are for students' reference, but appropriate variations or expansions are to be encouraged.

Ask questions like the following to present the pictures:

- What is this person's job?
- Where does a (teacher) work?
- What does a (teacher) do?
- Do you know a (waitress)?
- Are any of you (cashiers)?
- What does a (mechanic) wear?

The Pictures

1. police officer—keep the streets safe
2. fire fighter—put out fires
3. mail carrier—deliver the mail
4. bus driver—drive a bus
5. teacher—teach lessons
6. seamstress—sew clothes
7. housewife—take care of the house
8. cashier—take your money and give you change
9. secretary—work in an office
10. operator—help with phone calls
11. waitress/waiter—serve meals at a restaurant
12. dentist—take care of your teeth
13. janitor—clean buildings
14. security guard—watch stores
15. mechanic—fix cars
16. factory worker—work in a factory

Sample presentation, Picture 1: police officer

Today we're going to talk about jobs. What's a job? . . . Yes, it's your work. For example, what's *my* job? . . . Yes, I'm a teacher. Now, let's look at this first picture. Who is this? . . . Yes, it's Sue. And what does Sue do? Is she a police officer, or a teacher? . . . Yes. She's a police officer. . . . Yes, José, we also say "policeman" and "policewoman." They all have the same meaning. Now tell me, what color are a police officer's clothes? . . . Yes, a police officer wears blue clothes. And where does a police officer work? . . . Yes, a police officer works on the street. And what does a police officer do? Does she teach or keep the streets safe? . . . Yes, she keeps the streets safe. Do you know "safe"? . . . Yes, Roberto, it's the opposite of "dangerous." And when do you feel safe—during the day or at night? . . . Yes, me too. I feel safe during the day. And do you feel safe at home, or on a dark street? . . . Yes. I feel safe at home too.

UNIT 19: Your Family (page 117)

Presenting page 117
Start with "me" in the middle of page 117 and ask questions like the following to present the family tree:

- Who is this person?
- Do you have a (sister)?
- How many (sisters) do you have?
- What is/are your (sister's) name(s)?
- How old is/are your (sister)?
- Where do(es) your (sister) live?

Sample presentation: husband/wife/children

Today we're going to talk about people in our families. Let's start with me. Here [pointing]—do you see me? And this [pointing] is my husband—or wife, if I'm a man. This line [pointing] shows that we're married. Now you see we have one daughter [pointing] and one son [pointing]. What's a daughter? . . . Yes, a girl. And a son? . . . Yes, a son is a boy. So how many children [pointing to the word "children"] do we have? . . . Yes, we have two children. What are children? . . . Yes, children are sons and daughters. Now, Lee, how many sons do you have? . . . Oh, one son. And how many daughters? . . . Yes, two daughters. So, class, how many children does Lee have? . . . Yes, he has three children.

Presenting page 119

Point out "Jody" in the middle of page 119 and, choosing her relatives in random order, ask three questions about each person:

- What is Jody's (uncle's) name?
- How old is Jody's (uncle)?
- What does Jody's (uncle) do?

UNIT 20: What Do They Do? What Are They Doing? (page 123)

Teaching note: This unit contrasts present tense ("most summers") with present continuous ("this summer"). The students will be producing statements during the presentation as in the examples below. Allow several students to produce each of the statements and allow extra time for this presentation. Note that the activity on page 125 is not conversation practice, but rather listening practice for students to distinguish tense markers as they answer *your* questions.

Ask these questions about the kids' summers:

1. What do they usually do?
2. Where do they ride horses?
3. How long do they stay at camp?
4. Who do they go to camp with?
5. What kind of food do they eat there?

Answers

1. Ride horses.
2. At summer camp.
3. Three weeks.
4. Their classmates.
5. Terrible food.

Ask these questions about the kids this summer:

1. What are they doing?
2. Where are they camping?
3. How long are they staying in Alaska?
4. Who are they going with?
5. What kind of food are they eating?

Answers

1. Camping.
2. In Alaska.
3. Two weeks.
4. Their parents.
5. Barbecued hamburgers.

Ask these questions about Stan's summers:

1. What does he usually do in the summer?
2. Where does he relax?
3. How long does he stay there?
4. Who does he go with?
5. What kind of food does he eat there?

Answers

1. Relaxes.
2. At his mother's house.
3. One month.
4. His sister.
5. Spaghetti. (His mother loves spaghetti.)

Ask these questions about Stan this summer:

1. What's he doing?
2. Where is he playing golf?
3. How long is he staying in Hawaii?
4. Who is he going with?
5. What kind of food is he eating?

Answers

1. Playing golf.
2. In Hawaii.
3. Ten days.
4. Nobody. (He's alone.)
5. Seafood.

Sample presentation, Picture 1: the kids at summer camp

Today we're going to talk about summer activities. Who are these people [pointing]? . . . Yes, the kids, Tim and Kate. And this first group of pictures [indicating] is what the kids do most summers [pointing to the words "most summers"]. What does that mean, "most summers"? . . . Yes, it means "usually." Now what do the kids usually do in the summer? Do they drive cars, or ride horses? . . . Yes. They ride horses. What's a horse? . . . Yes, it's an animal. Where do the kids ride horses, at home, or at summer camp? . . . Yes. At summer camp [pointing to picture]. What's a summer camp? . . . Yes, it's in the summer. And do kids go to summer camp to study? . . . No way. They go to have fun. What do they do at summer camp? Yes, they swim. What else do they do at summer camp? . . . Yes, they play baseball. OK, and how long do Tim and Kate stay at camp [pointing to dates]? . . . Yes, they stay for three weeks. And who do they go with, their parents or their classmates? . . . Yes, they go with their classmates. Now, what kind of food do they eat? Do they eat good food [pointing to picture]? . . . No! They eat *terrible* food! What's "terrible"? . . . Yes, "terrible" means very very bad. Now, look at the picture and listen. [Slowly, pointing to individual parts of picture] Most summers the kids ride horses at summer camp for three weeks. They go with their classmates and eat terrible food. Now who can say that? . . . Ulises, you want to try? Go ahead . . .

UNIT 21: At the Doctor (page 129)

Teaching note: The vocabulary in this unit will be reinforced by having students respond physically to commands from you (through Total Physical Response [TPR]), rather than through picture-based conversation practice. Thus the pictures on pages 129 and 133 appear with captions.

To teach pages 129–130

Use page 129 to review and clarify the vocabulary by reading the words and having students repeat. Then introduce the four verbs at the top of page 130 (*touch, scratch, cover,* and *rub*). Finally, have the students close their books, stand, and respond to commands that combine these four verbs and the body parts from page 129, for example, "Touch your forehead," "Scratch your nose."

To teach pages 133-134

Introduce the vocabulary on page 133 through TPR *before* the students look at the page. Start by telling the students that you are (playing the role of) the doctor and they are patients. Have them stand and respond as you give the commands on page 133. Advance through the page slowly, item by item, and use simple variations to reinforce the verbs, for example, "Take off your shirt/hat/shoes" "Straighten your arm/leg/back." (Model pantomimed responses for such commands as "Take off your shirt" and "Lie on your stomach.") *Then* have students open their books to page 133 as you review the new vocabulary with them (Activity 8). In Activity 9 (page 133), the students will again stand and follow your commands, having now seen the words in print. (As an alternative, you can have students work in pairs, one reading the commands from page 133 and the other standing and responding.)

UNIT 22: What's the Matter with May? (page 135)

Teaching note: As in Unit 4, students will be asked a question during the presentation that is not answered in the book—"Why does this person have this problem?"—about which they are to speculate freely.

Ask questions like the following to present the pictures:

- What's the matter with this person?
- How do you know s/he has a (headache)?
- Why does s/he have a (headache)? (free speculation)
- Do you ever get a (headache)?
- Why/when do you have a (headache)?
- What do you do when you have a (headache)?

The Pictures

1. a headache/head hurts
2. a toothache/tooth hurts
3. an earache/ear hurts
4. a stomachache/stomach hurts
5. a backache/back hurts
6. a cold/the flu
7. a fever/a temperature
8. a cough
9. a sore throat/throat hurts
10. a rash
11. diarrhea
12. dizzy

Sample presentation, Picture 1: a headache

Today we're going to talk about when we're not feeling well. What does that mean—"not feeling well"? . . . Yes, it means we're sick, we have a problem with our body. And when someone isn't feeling well, we can ask them, "What's the matter?" For example, let's take a look at May here. Is May feeling well? . . . No, she isn't. Well then, what's the matter with May? . . . Yes, her head hurts. Or, we can say she has a headache. How do you know she has a headache? . . . Yes, she's touching her forehead. Now *why* do you think she has a headache? Any ideas? . . . You think she's been working too hard, Fernando? Well, that's one reason people get headaches. Any other ideas? . . . Yes, Zoe, maybe she has a headache because she has a cold. Do you ever get headaches? . . . You do sometimes, Ali? . . .

UNIT 23: What's Maria Going to Do Tomorrow? (page 141)

Teaching note: Proceed from one picture to the next (in the calendar) using the expression "the next day . . . " Do not introduce the time expressions on page 143 until after the vocabulary on pages 141–142 has been introduced and practiced. The future *going to* will be used in the presentation, but not formally introduced until page 142.

Ask questions like the following to present the pictures:

- What's Maria going to do (the next day)?
- When do we (pack a suitcase)?
- Where do we (play tennis)?
- Do/did you ever (climb a mountain)?
- When do/did you (play tennis)?
- Who did/do you (play golf) with?
- How often do you (go fishing.)?

The Pictures

July 11—pack
July 12—fly to Alaska
July 13—ride a horse
July 14—go fishing
July 15–16—play golf
July 17–18—climb a mountain
July 19—play tennis
July 20—fly back
July 21—unpack
July 22—see Stan

Sample presentation, Picture 1: pack

Today we're going to talk about Maria's summer plans. First, what do we have here? . . . Yes, it's a calendar. What month is it? . . . Yes, it's July. And what day is today? . . . Yes, today is July 10th. And Maria is going to take a trip this summer. What's a "trip"? . . . Yes, when you go away somewhere. Who took a trip last summer? . . . Oh, Julio, where did you take a trip to? . . . Disneyland? Well, Maria's going to take a trip to Alaska. You know where Alaska is [indicating classroom map of the United States]? . . . Yes, it's there [pointing to map]. What's Maria going to do tomorrow [indicating on calendar]? . . . Is she going to go fishing, or pack? . . . Yes, she's going to pack. What's this [pointing to suitcase]? . . . Yes, it's a suitcase. When do we use a suitcase? . . . Yes, when we take a trip. Do you have a suitcase, Anton? . . . You do? What color is your suitcase? . . . Brown? Oh, same as mine! Now then, what's Maria going to pack in her suitcase? . . . Yes, her clothes. What else is she going to pack? . . . Yes, her toothbrush. So tomorrow Maria's going to pack. And what's she going to do the next day? . . .

UNIT 24: What's Going to Happen Next Monday? (page 147)

Ask questions like the following to present the pictures:

- What's (Maria) going to do on (Monday)?
  or What's going to happen to (Maria) on (Monday)?
- Why is/isn't (she) going to (take the bus)?
- Do/did you ever (buy a new car)?
- When did you (buy a new car)?
- Do you like/want to (sleep all day)?

The Pictures

Maria
Mon.—get a ring
Tues.—get married
Wed.—*not* go to work

John
Mon.—get a raise
Tues.—buy a car
Wed.—*not* take the bus

The Kids
Mon.—make a mess.
Tues.—*not* clean their room
Wed.—get in trouble

Zabu
Mon.—eat all day
Tues.—sleep all day
Wed.—not do anything

Sample presentation: what Maria is going to do next week

Today John and Maria are talking to a fortune-teller [indicating the fortune-teller in the picture]. Do you know what a fortune-teller is? . . . Yes. She tells you about your future. For example, what does she tell you? Yes, if you're going to get married. And . . . ? Yes—if you're going to make a lot of money. Do you ever go to a fortune-teller? . . . You do, Juana? . . . And you don't Tamim? So you don't believe in fortune-tellers? Well, let's see what this fortune-teller is saying. First, let's look at Maria's fortune. What's going to happen to Maria next Monday [indicating in picture]? . . . Yes, she's going to get

a ring! Does anyone here have a ring? . . .Yes, you have a ring, Sally, and you have a ring, Rubens. Where do we wear rings, class? . . . Yes, we wear rings on our fingers. Now, what sometimes happens after someone gets a ring? . . . Yes, they get married. In fact, what's going to happen to Maria on Tuesday? . . . Sure enough! She's going to get married! And what about Wednesday? Is she going to go to work [indicating the big *X* in picture]? . . . No, she isn't. She isn't going to go to work the day after she gets married. Why isn't she going to go to work? . . . Yes, I suppose she will be on a honeymoon with her husband. Now let's see what's going to happen to John next week. . . .

UNIT 25: Can You Help Me, Please? (page 153)

Teaching note: If there is any doubt about your students understanding *can/can't,* precede the presentation by writing the two words on the chalkboard and clarifying them with a few easy examples, such as "Can I speak English? . . . Yes, I can." "Can I touch the ceiling [attempting to do so]? . . . No, I can't."

Presenting page 153
Ask questions like the following to present the pictures on page 153:

- What's the problem here?
- Why is this person having this problem?
- Do you ever have this problem?
- What do you do when you have this problem?
- What can you say to a friend with this problem?

The Pictures

1. can't open bottle/too tight—I can open it for you.
2. can't understand these directions—
   I can explain them for you.
3. can't reach that box—I can get it for you.
4. can't move this box/too heavy—
   I can help you move it.
5. can't start this machine—I can help you start it.
6. can't find the sugar—I can help you find it.

Sample presentation, Picture 1: can't open bottle/too tight

Today we're going to talk about having problems at work and asking for help. Take a look here. What's this woman holding? . . . Yes, a bottle. And what does she want to do? . . . Yes, she wants to open the bottle. But *can* she open the bottle? . . . No, she can't. Why can't she open the bottle? Is it too big, or too *tight* [pantomiming trying to open a tightly capped bottle]? . . . Yes. It's too tight. What else is sometimes too tight? . . . Is your belt sometimes too tight [pulling belt tight]? . . . Yes, belts are sometimes too tight. And do you sometimes hold your husband or wife tight [pantomiming this]? . . . Yes. And what else is sometimes too tight? . . . Yes, sometimes shoes are too tight [pantomiming]. What else? . . . Yes, sometimes a jar is too tight, and we can't open it [pantomiming]. Now, back to the picture. This woman can't open the bottle because it's too tight. If your friend at work has this problem, you can say, "I can open it for you." Can you say that? Try it, Heng. . . . Now you try it, Leticia: "I can open it for you." . . .

Presenting page 156

Ask questions like the following to present the pictures on page 156:

- What's the problem in this picture?
- How does this problem happen?
- Does this problem ever happen to you?
- Can you (change a tire)?
- What do you use to (change a tire)?

The Pictures

1. fix a broken dish
2. fix a leaking faucet
3. fix a broken window
4. fix a stopped-up sink
5. change a light bulb
6. change a tire

Sample presentation, Picture 1: fix a broken dish

Today I want to ask you about some little jobs at home—if you can do them or not. Let's take a look at this picture. What's this? . . . Yes, it's a dish. Where do we use dishes? . . . Yes, we use dishes in the kitchen. And why do we use dishes? . . . We use dishes to eat. Now, what happens if we drop a dish [pantomiming this, with the sound of a crash]? Yes, the dish breaks! Do you sometimes break a dish? . . . I see a lot of you do. Me too! Look at these two pictures [pointing]. Which dish is broken? . . . Yes, the one on the left is broken. Class, what does "broken" mean? . . . Yes, "broken" means it breaks. Now let me ask you, Kim, can you fix a broken dish? . . . You can? Good. Do you fix a broken dish with a hammer [pantomiming]? . . . No, you don't fix a broken dish with a hammer. You fix a broken dish with . . . Yes, you fix a broken dish with glue.

UNIT 26: Where Did Maria Go Yesterday? (page 159)

Teaching note: The places depicted in the calendar have all been previously introduced, so you will use this presentation to introduce the time expressions from page 160. The tense marker *did* will be used in the presentation but not formally introduced until page 161. Elicit short answers from students, as the irregular form *went* will not be formally introduced until Unit 27.

Sample presentation: August 23, 22, 21, and 20

Today we're going to talk about what places Maria went to this month. First, what do we have here? . . . Yes, it's another calendar. And what month is it? . . . It's August. And what's the date today [pointing to "today" in the calendar]? . . . Yes, today is August 24th. Now if this is today [pointing again], what day is this [pointing to Aug. 23]? . . . Yes, it's yesterday. And where did Maria go yesterday? . . . Yes, she went to a restaurant yesterday. Now, if this is yesterday [pointing again], then what day is this [pointing to Aug. 22]? . . . Yes. It's the day before yesterday. And where did Maria go the day before yesterday? . . . Yes, she went to the bank the day before yesterday. Now [pointing to Aug. 21], how many day ago was this day [counting backward from Aug. 24]? . . . Yes, it was three days ago. And this day [pointing to Aug. 20]? . . . Four days ago. And what about this [pointing to

Aug. 17]? . . . Yes. That was one week ago. Now [directing attention away from picture], what time was it one hour ago [looking at watch]? . . . Yes, one hour ago it was two fifteen. And what year was it ten years ago? . . . Very good, ten years ago it was 1985. Now [directing attention back to picture and pointing to Aug. 21], where did Maria go three days ago? . . . Yes, three days ago she went to the hospital. And what about four days ago? . . .

UNIT 27: What Did John Do Last Week? (page 165)

Teaching note: You will use the past tense *-ed* in your presentation, but students will not produce it until it is formally introduced on page 167.

Ask questions like the following to present the pictures:

- What did (John) do on (Tuesday)?
- Why did (he) (cough all day)? (free speculation)
- Do/did you ever (argue)?
- How often do you (cry)?
- When did you (cry)?
- Do you like to (rest in bed)?

The Pictures

John
Tues.—coughed all day
Wed.—called in sick
Thurs.—rested in bed

Maria and Stan
Tues.—argued
Wed.—cried
Thurs.—stayed home

May
Tues.—washed her hair
Wed.—danced all night
Thurs.—missed work

Zabu
Tues.—played with the kids
Wed.—barked at the mail carrier
Thurs.—didn't do anything

Sample presentation: what John did last week

Today we're going to talk about what people did last week. First let's look at John. What did he do last Tuesday? Remember this picture? . . . Yes, he coughed. In the morning? In the afternoon? When [indicating the sun]? . . . Yes, he coughed all day. It wasn't a good day for John. And what did he do on Wednesday? Did he go to work, or did he call in sick? . . . Yes, he called in sick. What does that mean, "called in sick"? Yes, he called his work. And what did he say? . . . Yes. He said he wasn't going to work that day because he was sick. Do you ever call in sick? . . . You do? When did you call in sick, Luisa? . . . Oh, you called in sick last Wednesday. So *that's* why you weren't in school! And did your boss get angry when you called in sick? . . . No? Well, you must have a nice boss. Now let's look at what John did on Thursday. . . .